Rotterdam

2024

Travel Guide

Your Essential Guide to Exploring the City's Wonders

Betty Vanslyke

Copyright © 2024 by Betty Vanslyke

All rights reserved. No part of this publication may be reproduced, distributed, or transmitted in any form or by any means, including photocopying, recording, or other electronic or mechanical methods, without the prior written permission of the publisher, except in the case of brief quotations embodied in critical reviews and certain other noncommercial uses permitted by copyright law.

HOW TO USE THIS GUIDE

Welcome to your comprehensive guide to exploring Rotterdam! Whether you're a first-time visitor or a seasoned traveler looking to uncover hidden gems, this guide is designed to help you make the most of your time in this dynamic city. Here's how to navigate through the wealth of information provided:

TABLE OF CONTENTS

Refer to the table of contents to find the information you need quickly and easily. Each chapter is organized to cover different aspects of your Rotterdam adventure, from must-see sights and top attractions to dining options and accommodation recommendations.

MAP OF ROTTERDAM

Use the map of Rotterdam provided in this guide to familiarize yourself with the city's layout and key landmarks. It's a handy tool for planning your itinerary and navigating your way around Rotterdam's streets and neighborhoods.

INTRODUCTION

Read the introduction to get a brief overview of what Rotterdam has to offer, from its innovative architecture and rich cultural scene to its culinary delights and essential travel tips.

CHAPTER ONE

Learn why Rotterdam should be your next adventure, discover the city's unique rhythm, and find practical advice on getting to and around Rotterdam. Dive into our neighborhood guide to uncover hidden gems and must-see attractions in each district.

CHAPTER TWO

Explore accommodation options in Rotterdam, including top hotels, family-friendly stays, budget-friendly choices, and vacation rentals. Find the perfect place to rest and rejuvenate during your Rotterdam getaway.

CHAPTER THREE

Discover the top attractions in Rotterdam, from iconic landmarks like the Markthal and Erasmus Bridge to cultural institutions such as the Maritime Museum and Museum Boijmans Van Beuningen. Explore Rotterdam's diverse neighborhoods and uncover the city's hidden gems.

CHAPTER FOUR

Embark on Rotterdam tours to delve deeper into the city's history, culture, and local secrets. Whether you prefer guided walking tours, bike excursions, or boat cruises, there's a tour for every interest and budget.

CHAPTER FIVE

Indulge your taste buds with our curated list of top restaurants in Rotterdam, ranging from fine dining establishments to local eateries and budget-friendly gems. Discover where to find delicious meals and refreshing drinks to suit every mood and occasion.

With this guide as your companion, you're ready to embark on an unforgettable journey through the vibrant streets and hidden treasures of Rotterdam. Let the adventure begin!

ROTTERDAM

TABLE OF CONTENT

HOW TO USE THIS GUIDE 2

TABLE OF CONTENT 6

MAP OF ROTTERDAM 10

INTRODUCTION 11

   Discover Rotterdam: Where Innovation Meets Tradition 11

   Must-See Sights in Rotterdam: A Blend of Modern Marvels and Historic Gems 14

   Savor Rotterdam: A Culinary Adventure Awaits 18

   Words and Phrases Every Tourist Should Know 23

CHAPTER ONE 27

   Ditch the Guidebooks: Why Rotterdam Should Be Your Next Adventure 27

   Rotterdam Rhythm: Finding Your Perfect Beat in This Dynamic City 29

   Conquering the Commute: Your Guide to Getting to Rotterdam, the Netherlands 32

   Rotterdam Revealed: A Neighborhood Guide for the Discerning Traveler 37

CHAPTER TWO... 42

Accommodation and Place to Stay in Rotterdam 42

Top Hotels in Rotterdam 42

The James Hotel Rotterdam 42

Savoy Hotel Rotterdam 44

nhow Rotterdam 45

Hotel New York 47

Room Mate Bruno 48

citizenM Rotterdam 50

CityHub Rotterdam 51

Holiday Inn Express Rotterdam - Central Station, an IHG Hotel 53

ss Rotterdam 55

Rotterdam Marriott Hotel 57

ibis Rotterdam City Centre Hotel 59

Family-Friendly Hotels in Rotterdam 60

Budget-Friendly Hotels in Rotterdam: Exploring the City Without Breaking the Bank 64

Vacation Rentals 68

CHAPTER THREE 74

Top Attractions in Rotterdam 74

Markthal (Market Hall) 74

Cube Houses (Kijk-Kubus) 77

Erasmus Bridge (Erasmusbrug) 80

The Rotterdam (formerly SS Rotterdam) 84

De Rotterdam (Skyscraper) 87

Delfshaven 91

Sint Laurenskerk (St. Lawrence Church) 95

Maritime Museum Rotterdam 99

Kunsthal Rotterdam.. 103

Museum Boijmans Van Beuningen.. 107

Het Park 111

Kinderdijk Windmills... 115

CHAPTER FOUR.. 120

Rotterdam Tours to Uncover the City's Hidden Gems and Must-See Sights 120

CHAPTER FIVE 126

Top Restaurants in Rotterdam 126

Fine Dining Restaurants in Rotterdam 126

Local Eats Gems You Won't Want to Miss...................................... 130

Bites That Won't Break the Bank... 135

Deliciously Cheap Eats You Can't Miss! 139

Bars & Pubs for Every Mood... 144

CHAPTER SIX.. 149

Day Trips from Rotterdam 149

Delft 149

The Hague 150

Kinderdijk.. 150

Gouda 151

CONCLUSION **152**

Unveiling Rotterdam's Unforgettable Spirit............................ 152

ROTTERDAM

MAP OF ROTTERDAM

https://www.google.com/maps/d/edit?mid=1qZPqHX9JgdFUg42kDOD_CxzBCjFe8cA&ll=51.930125765359435%2C4.4908281000000105&z=13

Scan the QR Code for Map of Rotterdam

INTRODUCTION

Discover Rotterdam: Where Innovation Meets Tradition

Welcome to Rotterdam, a city that defies expectations and embraces innovation at every turn. Situated in the heart of the Netherlands, Rotterdam is a vibrant metropolis renowned for its bold architecture, dynamic culture, and pioneering spirit. From its iconic skyline punctuated by modern skyscrapers to its historic waterfront dotted with centuries-old windmills, Rotterdam offers a captivating blend of old-world charm and contemporary allure that beckons travelers from around the globe.

A City Reborn: Once ravaged by war and natural disasters, Rotterdam has risen from the ashes to become a beacon of resilience and reinvention. Following the devastation of World War II, Rotterdam embarked on a remarkable journey of reconstruction and renewal, reshaping its urban landscape with bold architectural visions and forward-thinking urban planning. Today, the city stands as a testament to the power of innovation and the enduring spirit of its inhabitants.

Architectural Marvels: Step into the future with Rotterdam's cutting-edge architecture, where sleek skyscrapers and avant-garde designs redefine the city skyline. From the iconic Erasmus Bridge and the daring Cube Houses to the shimmering towers of De Rotterdam and the innovative Markthal, Rotterdam's architectural wonders captivate the imagination and push the boundaries of design innovation.

Cultural Kaleidoscope: Immerse yourself in Rotterdam's vibrant cultural scene, where art, music, and creativity flourish in every corner of the city. Explore world-class museums such as the Kunsthal and Museum Boijmans Van Beuningen, showcasing masterpieces from across the ages. Experience the eclectic energy of Witte de Withstraat, Rotterdam's cultural hub, where galleries, theaters, and trendy cafes converge to create a dynamic atmosphere buzzing with creativity.

Gateway to the World: As Europe's largest port city, Rotterdam has long been a global hub of trade, commerce, and cultural exchange. Wander through the historic Delfshaven neighborhood, where cobblestone streets and centuries-old canals evoke the city's maritime heritage. Marvel at the Kinderdijk windmills, a UNESCO World Heritage site, and witness the ingenuity of Dutch water management firsthand.

Innovative Spirit: Get inspired by Rotterdam's entrepreneurial spirit and cutting-edge initiatives in sustainability, technology, and urban development. Explore the innovative Rotterdam Science Tower, a hub for research and innovation at the forefront of scientific discovery. Experience the city's commitment to sustainability with initiatives such as the Floating Pavilion and the Rotterdam Climate Initiative, which aim to create a more resilient and environmentally-friendly urban environment.

A Feast for the Senses: Indulge your taste buds with Rotterdam's diverse culinary scene, where traditional Dutch cuisine meets international flavors from around the world. Sample fresh seafood at the bustling Markthal, savor artisanal cheeses at local markets, or dine al fresco at waterfront restaurants overlooking the scenic River Maas.

Adventure Awaits: Whether you're exploring the city's hidden gems by bicycle, cruising along the canals by boat, or simply soaking in the vibrant atmosphere of Rotterdam's lively streets, adventure awaits around every corner. Discover the magic of Rotterdam, where innovation meets tradition and every experience is an invitation to explore, discover, and be inspired. Welcome to Rotterdam – where the future begins today.

Must-See Sights in Rotterdam: A Blend of Modern Marvels and Historic Gems

Rotterdam, a phoenix risen from the ashes of WWII, boasts a unique cityscape where bold, modern architecture mingles with remnants of its rich history.

Here's a guide to must-see sights that capture the essence of this dynamic Dutch city:

Architectural Wonders:

- **Markthal (Market Hall):** This horseshoe-shaped indoor market is a feast for the senses. Marvel at the vibrant stained-glass artwork on the ceiling while browsing stalls overflowing with fresh produce, flowers, and local delicacies.

- **Cube Houses (Kijk-Kubus):** These quirky tilted houses are Rotterdam's architectural icons. Take a guided tour inside one or simply snap photos from outside to capture their unique perspective.

- **Erasmus Bridge (Erasmusbrug):** Soaring over the Maas River, this impressive cable-stayed bridge is a symbol of Rotterdam's modern skyline. Take a walk or bike ride across the bridge for panoramic city views.

- **The Rotterdam (formerly SS Rotterdam):** Step aboard this historic ocean liner turned museum. Explore its decks, cabins, and engine room, and learn about its fascinating history as a passenger ship.

- **De Rotterdam (skyscraper):** Ascend to the top of the Netherlands' tallest building for breathtaking 360-degree views of the city. This architectural marvel exemplifies Rotterdam's modern aesthetic.

Historical Gems:

- **Delfshaven:** Explore this charming 17th-century harbor district, where the Pilgrim Fathers set sail for America in 1620. Stroll along the canal, visit the historic ships, and soak in the area's maritime heritage.

- **Sint Laurenskerk (St. Lawrence Church):** This Gothic church, one of the few structures to survive the wartime bombings, boasts a beautiful interior and a climbable tower offering panoramic city views.

- **Maritime Museum Rotterdam:** Delve into Rotterdam's rich maritime history at this interactive museum. Explore historic ships, learn about the port's development, and witness fascinating exhibitions about the seafaring world.

Cultural Delights:

- **Kunsthal:** This contemporary art museum showcases a diverse collection of modern and temporary exhibitions. Immerse yourself in the world of innovative art, design, and architecture.

- **Museum Boijmans Van Beuningen:** Housing an impressive collection of Dutch masters and European art, this museum is a treat for art lovers. Admire works by Rembrandt, Bruegel, and Monet, among others.

- **Het Park:** Escape the urban bustle in this sprawling park. Rent a paddleboat and explore the canals, have a picnic on the lawns, or visit the verdant arboretum, offering a peaceful oasis in the city center.

Beyond the City Center:

- **Kinderdijk Windmills:** Take a day trip to Kinderdijk, a UNESCO World Heritage Site. Witness a row of 19 iconic windmills, perfectly preserved and still operational, offering a glimpse into Dutch history and engineering marvels.

Bonus Tip: Purchase a Rotterdam Welcome Card for discounted entry to many attractions, unlimited public transportation use, and special offers at restaurants and shops.

This list provides a starting point for your Rotterdam adventure. With its blend of modern marvels, historical gems, and cultural delights, Rotterdam offers something for everyone. So lace up your walking shoes, grab your camera, and get ready to explore this captivating city!

Savor Rotterdam: A Culinary Adventure Awaits

Welcome to Rotterdam, a city where culinary innovation thrives and every meal is an unforgettable experience.

From hearty Dutch classics to international delights, Rotterdam's diverse food scene offers a tantalizing array of flavors, textures, and aromas that will delight your taste buds and leave you craving for more. Get ready to embark on a gastronomic journey through Rotterdam's vibrant streets and discover why this city is a food lover's paradise.

Dutch Delights: Start your culinary exploration with a taste of traditional Dutch cuisine, where hearty dishes and comforting flavors reign supreme. Indulge in a steaming bowl of erwtensoep (pea soup) or stamppot (mashed potatoes with vegetables), served piping hot and garnished with savory meats. Sample the iconic Dutch delicacy, bitterballen, crispy fried meatballs filled with rich, savory gravy that pair perfectly with a cold pint of local beer.

Global Flavors: Venture beyond Dutch borders and immerse yourself in Rotterdam's vibrant international food scene, where flavors from around the world converge to create a melting pot of culinary delights. Explore the bustling streets of Witte de Withstraat, where trendy cafes and multicultural eateries serve up everything from authentic Thai street food to mouthwatering Middle

Eastern mezze. Indulge in flavorful Indonesian rijsttafel (rice table) or savor the exotic spices of Moroccan tagines, transporting your taste buds on a culinary journey across continents.

Seafood Sensations: As Europe's largest port city, Rotterdam boasts an abundance of fresh seafood sourced directly from the North Sea. Dive into a platter of haring (herring), a Dutch delicacy enjoyed raw with onions and pickles, or feast on a bounty of briny oysters, succulent mussels, and plump shrimp at the city's seafood markets and waterfront restaurants. Don't miss the opportunity to sample kibbeling, crispy battered fish bites served piping hot with tangy tartar sauce, a beloved Dutch street food favorite.

Artisanal Eats: Experience Rotterdam's burgeoning artisanal food scene, where local producers and passionate chefs showcase their culinary creativity and commitment to quality ingredients. Explore the city's vibrant food markets, such as the Markthal and Fenix Food Factory, where you can sample a diverse selection of artisanal cheeses, freshly baked bread, handcrafted chocolates, and locally sourced meats. Treat yourself to a gourmet dining experience at one of Rotterdam's

Michelin-starred restaurants, where innovative chefs push the boundaries of culinary excellence with imaginative dishes that celebrate the best of Dutch and international cuisine.

Craft Beverages: Quench your thirst with Rotterdam's craft beverage scene, where artisanal breweries, hipster coffee shops, and chic cocktail bars cater to every palate. Sip on a locally brewed IPA or a refreshing Witbier at one of the city's craft beer bars, where you can sample an ever-changing lineup of innovative brews from Rotterdam's burgeoning craft beer scene. Indulge in a velvety espresso or a perfectly crafted cappuccino at a cozy coffee house, or unwind with a creative cocktail crafted with premium spirits and seasonal ingredients at a trendy rooftop bar overlooking the city skyline.

Sweet Temptations: No culinary journey through Rotterdam would be complete without indulging in some sweet treats to satisfy your cravings. Indulge your sweet tooth with a slice of Dutch apple pie topped with a dollop of freshly whipped cream, or sample stroopwafels, thin waffle cookies filled with gooey caramel syrup that are perfect for dipping in your morning coffee. Treat yourself to a scoop of artisanal gelato or a decadent slice of cake at one of Rotterdam's charming patisseries and dessert shops, where every bite is a celebration of sweetness and indulgence.

Food Festivals and Events: Experience Rotterdam's vibrant culinary culture firsthand by attending one of the city's food festivals and events, where local chefs, food artisans, and gastronomic enthusiasts come together to celebrate the best of Rotterdam's food and drink scene. From street food festivals and beer tastings to gourmet food markets and culinary competitions, there's always something delicious happening in Rotterdam that will tempt your taste buds and leave you craving for more.

Explore, Indulge, Repeat: Whether you're a culinary connoisseur or simply love to eat, Rotterdam offers a world of flavors and experiences waiting to be discovered. So grab your fork and join us on a culinary adventure through the streets of Rotterdam, where every meal is a celebration of flavor, creativity, and community. From traditional Dutch classics to global gastronomic delights, Rotterdam invites you to savor every bite and indulge in the rich tapestry of flavors that make this city a true food lover's paradise. Bon appétit!

Words and Phrases Every Tourist Should Know

Here are some essential words and phrases every tourist should know in Dutch, along with pronunciations (written approximately in English sounds):

Greetings and Basic Courtesy:

- **Hallo (Ha-लो)**: Hello

- **Dag (Dakh):** Goodbye (informal)

- **Doei (Doy):** Goodbye (very informal)

- **Dank u wel (Dahnk yoo vell):** Thank you

- **Graag gedaan (Grahkh heh-dahn):** You're welcome

- **Alstublieft (Al-stoo-bleeft):** Please (formal)

- **Excuseer mij (Ex-coos měy):** Excuse me

Getting Around:

- **Ja (Yah):** Yes

- **Nee (Nay):** No

- **Sorry (Sor-ri):** Sorry (also used to get someone's attention)

- **Waar is (Vahr ees):** Where is

- **Toilet (トイレット Toiretoreto (Japanese) or WC (ヴェーセー Veesee (Japanese)):** Toilet (Many places might have signs in English or Japanese for tourists)

- **Station (Stah-syon):** Station

- **Hoeveel kost dit? (Hoe-veel kost dit?):** How much does this cost?

- **Kan ik u helpen? (Kan ik yoo helpen?):** Can I help you?

Numbers (1-10):

- Een (Ayn) - One

- Twee (Tvay) - Two

- Drie (Dree) - Three

- Vier (Vee-er) - Four

- Vijf (Veyf) - Five

- Zes (Zes) - Six

- Zeven (Zay-ven) - Seven

- Acht (Acht) - Eight

- Negen (Nay-ghen) - Nine

- Tien (Tee-en) - Ten

Food and Drinks:

- **Bier (Bee-er):** Beer

- **Water (Vah-ter):** Water

- **Koffie (Kof-fie):** Coffee

- **Thee (Tsay):** Tea

- **Eten (Ay-ten):** Food

- **Restaurant (Res-toh-rahnt):** Restaurant

- **Bar (Bar):** Bar

Phrases:

- **Ik spreek geen Nederlands (Ik spraak geen Nederlands) (Ik speak geen Nay-der-lants):** I don't speak Dutch.

- **Spreek je Engels? (Spraak je Engels?) (Speak ye Eng-els?):** Do you speak English?

- **Kun je langzamer praten? (Kun je lahng-zah-mer prah-ten?):** Can you speak slower?

Bonus:

- **Proost (Proost):** Cheers!

Tips:

- A smile and kind gestures go a long way, even if you don't speak perfect Dutch.

- Many people in tourist areas will understand basic English.

- Learning a few key phrases shows respect for the local culture.

- There are many translation apps available to help you communicate.

CHAPTER ONE

Ditch the Guidebooks: Why Rotterdam Should Be Your Next Adventure

Forget the usual suspects of Amsterdam and Bruges. Rotterdam is the bold, unexpected city that will steal your travel heart. Here's why this dynamic Dutch metropolis should be at the top of your travel bucket list:

A City Reborn: Rotterdam isn't your typical European city. Rise above the ordinary and explore a cityscape where innovative architecture like the cube houses and Erasmus Bridge mingles with remnants of a rich history. Walk in the footsteps of resilience as you witness Rotterdam's transformation from a city ravaged by WWII to a beacon of modern design.

A Feast for the Senses: Indulge your inner foodie in a city where flavors go global. Sample fresh produce and international delicacies at the architecturally stunning Markthal. Savor succulent seafood at a harborside restaurant with panoramic views. Embark on a culinary adventure through bustling streets, where Indonesian curries mingle with fragrant Vietnamese pho. Rotterdam's food scene is a vibrant tapestry reflecting its multicultural heritage.

A Cultural Powerhouse: Beyond the delicious food, Rotterdam pulsates with artistic energy. Delve into the world of contemporary art at the Kunsthal, or step aboard the SS Rotterdam, a historic ocean liner transformed into a fascinating maritime museum. Catch a performance at a renowned theater, or soak up local vibes at trendy cafes with outdoor terraces. Rotterdam's cultural scene offers something for every taste, from history buffs to art enthusiasts.

A Haven for Adventure Seekers: Rotterdam is more than just museums and architecture. Take a thrilling RIB speedboat tour through the bustling harbor, or explore the historic canals on a relaxing water taxi ride. Venture beyond the city center to Kinderdijk, a UNESCO World Heritage Site where rows of iconic windmills stand sentinel to Dutch ingenuity. Rotterdam offers a variety of experiences for the adrenaline junkie and the leisure traveler alike.

A City for Everyone: Rotterdam caters to all budgets and travel styles. Explore charming neighborhoods on foot, or hop on the efficient public transport system that whisks you to every corner of the city. Families will love the interactive museums and verdant parks, while history buffs can delve into the city's past. So ditch the crowds and discover a city that's authentic, exciting, and unlike anywhere else in Europe.

Rotterdam is a city that surprises and inspires. It's a place where the past, present, and future collide in a symphony of bold design, cultural richness, and a never-give-up spirit. Are you ready to experience its magic?

Rotterdam Rhythm: Finding Your Perfect Beat in This Dynamic City

Rotterdam, a city that pulsates with energy, offers a unique experience throughout the year. But when is the perfect time for you to visit this captivating Dutch metropolis? Let's explore the rhythm of Rotterdam and find the beat that matches your travel style:

Spring Awakening (March-May):

- **Pros:** Pleasant weather with blooming flowers and fewer crowds compared to summer.

- **Cons:** Occasional rain showers.

- **Perfect for:** Budget-conscious travelers and those who enjoy exploring at a leisurely pace. Catch events like the International Film Festival Rotterdam (IFFR) in January/February.

Summer Sizzle (June-August):

- **Pros:** Warmest weather, ideal for outdoor activities and soaking up the vibrant city life. Numerous festivals and events liven up the city.

- **Cons:** Peak tourist season with potentially higher prices and larger crowds.

- **Perfect for:** Festival enthusiasts and those who enjoy sunshine and long days. Experience events like the Rotterdam Street Art Festival (STRAAT) or the World Port Days.

Autumnal Delights (September-November):

- **Pros:** Milder temperatures with beautiful fall foliage. Fewer crowds and potentially lower hotel rates.

- **Cons:** Increased chances of rain and shorter daylight hours.

- **Perfect for:** Art lovers and those who enjoy cozy cafes and museums. Rotterdam celebrates Museum Week in October, offering free or discounted entry to many museums.

Winter Wonderland (December-February):

- **Pros:** Enchanting Christmas markets and festive decorations. Unique opportunity to experience the city with a magical winter ambiance.

- **Cons:** Coldest weather with potential rain or snow. Some outdoor attractions may have limited hours.

- **Perfect for:** Budget travelers (flights and hotels can be cheaper) and those who enjoy festive experiences. Embrace the winter cheer at the Rotterdam Christmas Market or enjoy ice skating on special rinks throughout the city.

Beyond the Seasons:

- **Events:** Rotterdam boasts a vibrant event calendar year-round. Check for specific concerts, exhibitions, or festivals that align with your interests and plan your trip accordingly.

- **Personal Preferences:** Consider your tolerance for crowds and weather when making your decision. Do you crave sunshine or prefer crisp autumn air?

Rotterdam's rhythm caters to all travelers. So, lace up your walking shoes, pack your bags, and get ready to experience the city that moves to its own beat. No matter when you visit, Rotterdam promises a unique and unforgettable adventure.

Conquering the Commute: Your Guide to Getting to Rotterdam, the Netherlands

Rotterdam, a city brimming with bold architecture, delectable food, and captivating culture, beckons you to explore its vibrant streets. But how do you get there? Fear not, intrepid traveler! This guide equips you with all the knowledge needed to navigate your journey to Rotterdam:

ROTTERDAM

Taking Flight:

- **Main Airport:** Rotterdam The Hague Airport (RTM) offers convenient connections to various European destinations. For a wider range of international flights, consider Amsterdam Schiphol Airport (AMS), a short train journey away.

- **Tips:** Book your flights well in advance, especially during peak season, to secure the best deals. Utilize flight comparison websites to find the most affordable options.

Seafaring Sojourn:

- **Ferry Connections:** For a unique travel experience, consider arriving by ferry from neighboring countries like the UK (Hull) or Belgium (Zeebrugge). Enjoy the scenic views and relax on board before docking in the heart of Rotterdam's bustling port.

- **Tips:** Research ferry routes and schedules in advance, especially during peak travel times. Consider booking a cabin for added comfort and privacy on longer journeys.

Train Travel Triumph:

- **Dutch Rail Network:** The Netherlands boasts an excellent and efficient railway system. Catch a train from major European cities like Paris, Brussels, or Berlin for a comfortable and scenic journey to Rotterdam Centraal Station, conveniently located in the city center.

- **Tips:** Purchase tickets online or at train stations. Consider Eurail or Interrail passes for extended travel through Europe. Download train schedule apps for convenient route planning and real-time updates.

Hitting the Road:

- **Motorway Network:** Rotterdam is easily accessible by car via a well-developed motorway network connecting it to other Dutch cities and neighboring countries.

- **Tips:** Research car rental options and parking availability in Rotterdam, as city center parking can be limited. Be aware of potential tolls on some motorways, especially when crossing borders.

Ensure you have the appropriate driving permits and documentation.

Sustainable Solutions:

- **Long-Distance Biking:** For the adventurous traveler, consider cycling to Rotterdam from nearby European destinations. Well-maintained cycling paths throughout the Netherlands make this a viable and eco-friendly option.

- **Tips:** Plan your route carefully, taking into account rest stops and terrain. Ensure your bike is in good working condition and invest in proper safety gear.

Beyond the Arrival:

- **Public Transportation:** Rotterdam boasts a fantastic public transport system with trams, metros, and buses, making it easy to get around the city. Purchase a Rotterdam Welcome Card for discounted travel and free entry to several attractions.

- **Taxis:** Taxis are readily available for convenient point-to-point travel, especially with luggage or after late-night outings. Download taxi hailing apps for ease of use.

Rotterdam awaits, a vibrant tapestry of experiences waiting to be unraveled. Choose your mode of transportation, pack your sense of adventure, and get ready to conquer the commute. This dynamic Dutch city promises a smooth arrival and an unforgettable adventure!

Rotterdam Revealed: A Neighborhood Guide for the Discerning Traveler

Rotterdam, a phoenix risen from the ashes of WWII, boasts a diverse tapestry of neighborhoods, each with its own unique character. Forget cookie-cutter districts – here's your guide to navigating Rotterdam's vibrant energy, no matter your travel style:

Culture Vulture's Paradise: Centrum (City Center):

- The beating heart of Rotterdam. Immerse yourself in iconic architecture like the Cube Houses and the Erasmus Bridge.

- Explore world-class museums like Kunsthal and Kunsthal 48, showcasing innovative contemporary art.

- Catch a performance at the renowned LantarenVenster theater or browse the Markthal, an architectural marvel brimming with fresh produce and international delicacies.

Hipster Haven: Witte de Withstraat:

- A trendy district teeming with independent art galleries, quirky shops, and vintage stores.

- Fuel up at a cozy cafe with outdoor seating and people-watch the vibrant street scene.

- Explore street art installations and hidden gems tucked away on side streets.

- By night, the area transforms into a lively hub, with trendy bars and alternative music venues attracting a young crowd.

Family Fun: Kralingen-Crooswijk:

- A charming and green neighborhood with a relaxed vibe.

- Perfect for families with its spacious parks like Kralingse Plas ideal for picnics, boating, and cycling.

- Explore the leafy streets lined with beautiful houses and visit the Rotterdam Zoo, a delightful haven for animal lovers of all ages.

History Buff's Bonanza: Delfshaven:

- A historic harbor district steeped in maritime history.

- Stroll along the picturesque canals and admire the 17th-century architecture.

- Visit the Pilgrim Fathers Church, where a group of religious separatists worshipped before sailing to America on the Mayflower.

- Sample traditional Dutch cuisine at waterfront restaurants with stunning harbor views.

Off the Beaten Path: Noordereiland:

- A unique island neighborhood offering a tranquil escape from the city center.

- Explore the leafy streets and historic warehouses converted into art studios and creative workspaces.

- Enjoy panoramic cityscapes from the Wilhelminaplein square.

- Take a ferry to nearby Katendrecht, a former docklands area now undergoing a trendy transformation, with hip bars and restaurants housed in old warehouses.

Beyond the Trendy Districts:

- **Feijenoord:** A multicultural neighborhood with a working-class vibe, undergoing exciting development.

- **Charlois & IJsselmonde:** Family-friendly areas with green spaces and a local atmosphere.

- **Hillegersberg:** A peaceful and affluent suburb with beautiful houses and leafy streets.

Rotterdam's neighborhoods are a kaleidoscope of experiences. From the bustling city center to the hidden gems off the beaten path, there's a place to suit every traveler's desire. So, ditch the tourist map, pick your Rotterdam persona, and embark on an adventure through this dynamic city's unique districts!

CHAPTER TWO

Accommodation and Place to Stay in Rotterdam

Top Hotels in Rotterdam

The James Hotel Rotterdam

Location: Aert van Nesstraat 25, 3012 CA Rotterdam The Netherlands

Price per night: From $66

Description: Unwind in comfortable luxury at The James, a stylish design hotel in the heart of Rotterdam. This three-star hotel offers a laid-back vibe with a focus on modern design and sustainability.

Amenities: While The James doesn't have its own restaurant or bar, it features a 24/7 food market for convenient snacks and drinks. The hotel prioritizes guest comfort with amenities like a gym, a meeting room, and a 24-hour front desk. To help you explore the city, they provide a complimentary city map highlighting their favorite hotspots.

Nearby Attractions: The James' central location makes it ideal for exploring Rotterdam on foot. Stroll down vibrant streets like Coolsingel, Meent, and Lijnbaan. The hotel is situated close to the Markthal Rotterdam, a must-see indoor market, and a short distance from Rotterdam Central Station for easy access to public transportation.

Why it's Perfect for Travelers: Budget-minded travelers looking for a comfortable and stylish stay in the heart of the city will love The James. Its central location allows for easy exploration and its focus on sustainability aligns with eco-conscious travelers. The friendly staff and complimentary city map are ideal for those who want to experience Rotterdam like a local.

Savoy Hotel Rotterdam

Location: Hoogstraat 81, 3011 PJ Rotterdam The Netherlands

Price per night: From $106

Description: Embrace the city's energy at the Savoy Hotel Rotterdam, a recently renovated hotel boasting a retro-chic interior inspired by the 1960s. This 4-star hotel offers a comfortable and stylish base to explore Rotterdam's vibrant scene.

Amenities: Guests can unwind in the hotel's casual bar or enjoy a drink on the terrace. Breakfast is available to fuel your day of adventures. The hotel offers free Wi-Fi throughout the property and room service for ultimate convenience.

Nearby Attractions: The Savoy Hotel's central location places you steps away from the hip Hoogkwartier neighborhood. Explore the nearby Market Hall, a haven for fresh produce and local delicacies. The famous Cube Houses and Old Harbor are also within walking distance.

Why it's Perfect for Travelers:

- **Design Enthusiasts:** The hotel's unique 1960s-inspired décor offers a stylish stay for design lovers.

- **Central Location:** Explore Rotterdam with ease - the hotel is close to public transport and major attractions.

- **Good Value:** The Savoy Hotel provides a comfortable and stylish stay at a competitive price point.

nhow Rotterdam

Location: Wilhelminakade 137, 3072 AP Rotterdam The Netherlands

Phone: 009 1 212-245-5462

Price per night: From 105

Description: Immerse yourself in art and design at nhow Rotterdam, a striking waterfront hotel housed in the iconic De Rotterdam building. This 4-star hotel, designed by renowned architect Rem Koolhaas, offers a unique blend of contemporary style and artistic flair.

Amenities: Be pampered at nhow's renowned rooftop bar and terrace, boasting breathtaking city views. Savor delicious cuisine at the hotel's restaurant, Elvy. For those traveling for work, nhow offers well-equipped meeting spaces and a business center.

Nearby Attractions: nhow Rotterdam's Wilhelmina Pier location places you directly on the waterfront. Explore the nearby Maritime Museum Rotterdam or stroll through the bustling Market Hall. Take a scenic boat tour or simply relax and enjoy the vibrant harbor atmosphere.

Why It's Perfect For Travelers:

- **Art and Design Aficionados:** nhow Rotterdam is an artistic haven, showcasing contemporary art and design throughout the hotel.

- **Waterfront Location:** Enjoy stunning city and river views and easy access to the harbor area.

- **Foodies and Nightlife Enthusiasts:** Indulge in delectable cuisine at Elvy and unwind at the popular rooftop bar.

Hotel New York

Location: Koninginnenhoofd 1, 3072 AD Rotterdam The Netherlands

Price per night: From 129

Description: Steep yourself in history and maritime charm at Hotel New York, a luxurious 4-star hotel housed in the former headquarters of the Holland-America Line. This iconic landmark offers a unique blend of historic grandeur and modern comfort.

Amenities: Guests can embark on a culinary journey at the hotel's various restaurants, or relax with a drink in the NYC Bar. Unwind in the hotel's spa or stay active in the fitness center. For special occasions, Hotel New York boasts stunning event spaces and even a traditional barbershop.

Nearby Attractions: Located in the Kop van Zuid district, Hotel New York is surrounded by trendy restaurants, bars, and shops. Explore the SS Rotterdam, a historic ocean liner turned museum, docked right next door. Take a scenic ferry ride across the river or visit the nearby Kunsthal Rotterdam, a renowned contemporary art museum.

Why It's Perfect For Travelers:

- **History Buffs:** Immerse yourself in Rotterdam's maritime history within the walls of this beautifully restored landmark.

- **Foodies and Bar Hoppers:** Savor delicious cuisine and creative cocktails at the hotel's various restaurants and bars.

- **Couples and Special Occasions:** Hotel New York's elegant ambiance and event spaces make it ideal for romantic getaways and special celebrations.

Room Mate Bruno

Location: 52 Wilhelminakade, 3072 AR Rotterdam The Netherlands

Visit hotel website

Phone: 108929580

Price per night: From $102

Description: Room Mate Bruno offers a characterful stay in Rotterdam. This 4-star boutique hotel, housed in a former Dutch East India Company tea warehouse, combines historic charm with modern design.

Amenities: Unwind in the hotel's sauna or steam room after a day of exploring. Work out in the fitness center or relax with a drink at the bar/lounge. The hotel also offers room service for ultimate convenience.

Nearby Attractions: Room Mate Bruno boasts a prime location in the Feijenoord district. The hotel is situated right across the street from the cruise terminal and within walking distance of the Wilhelminaplein metro and tram station, offering easy access to the city center. Explore the nearby Fenix Food Factory, a vibrant food hall offering a global selection of cuisines, or take a stroll along the Maas River.

Why It's Perfect For Travelers:

- **History Buffs:** Appreciate the hotel's unique location in a historic building, once a key part of Rotterdam's maritime trade.

- **Location, Location, Location:** Enjoy easy access to public transportation, the city center, and the waterfront area.

- **Foodies and Socializers:** Savor international flavors at the nearby Fenix Food Factory or unwind with a drink at the hotel's bar/lounge.

citizenM Rotterdam

Location: Gelderseplein 50, 3011 WZ Rotterdam The Netherlands

Price per night: From $105

Description: Experience a tech-savvy and stylish stay at citizenM Rotterdam, a modern hotel ideally situated in the heart of the city. This hotel is part of a well-known citizenM chain known for its innovative approach to hospitality.

Amenities: citizenM Rotterdam prioritizes convenience and comfort. Guests can enjoy high-speed Wi-Fi throughout the property, perfect for staying connected. The hotel offers self-service check-in/out kiosks for a quick and efficient arrival. Each compact room features a MoodPad, a tablet controlling the room's lighting, temperature, and even blinds.

Nearby Attractions: citizenM's prime location in the Oude Haven (Old Harbor) puts you steps away from

Rotterdam's vibrant center. Explore the nearby Cube Houses, a unique architectural landmark, or visit the Markthal, a stunning indoor market. Take a scenic boat tour on the historic harbor or delve into Rotterdam's rich maritime history at the Maritime Museum.

Why It's Perfect For Travelers:

- **Tech-Savvy Travelers:** CitizenM embraces technology, offering self-service options and in-room MoodPad control.

- **Location:** Immerse yourself in the heart of Rotterdam, with easy access to must-see sights and exciting neighborhoods.

- **Budget-Conscious Travelers:** CitizenM provides a comfortable and stylish stay at a competitive price point, ideal for budget-minded explorers.

CityHub Rotterdam

Location: Witte de Withstraat 87, 3012 BN Rotterdam The Netherlands

Price per night: $89

Description: CityHub Rotterdam is an urban hotel designed for the modern, social traveler. This trendy hostel offers a capsule hotel experience, perfect for budget-conscious adventurers seeking a comfortable and central location.

Amenities: CityHub prioritizes social interaction and convenience. Guests can connect and relax in the communal lounge areas. Shared, modern bathrooms and showers provide a clean and efficient experience. Free Wi-Fi keeps you connected, and the on-site self-service bar allows you to grab drinks and snacks at your leisure.

Nearby Attractions: CityHub Rotterdam boasts a prime location on Witte de Withstraat, a trendy street known for its vibrant nightlife, art galleries, and cool shops. Explore the nearby Kunsthal Rotterdam, a renowned contemporary art museum, or visit the Markthal, a stunning indoor market. Take a stroll along the Maas River or delve into Rotterdam's rich history at the Maritime Museum.

Why It's Perfect For Travelers:

- **Budget-Conscious Backpackers:** CityHub offers a comfortable and affordable stay in a central location, ideal for budget travelers.

- **Social Butterflies:** The communal areas and trendy location encourage interaction with fellow travelers.

- **Nightlife Enthusiasts:** Witte de Withstraat offers a lively bar and club scene right on your doorstep.

- **Location:** Immerse yourself in the heart of Rotterdam's cool and happening scene, with easy access to major attractions.

Holiday Inn Express Rotterdam - Central Station, an IHG Hotel

Location: Weena 121, 3013 CK Rotterdam The Netherlands

Phone: 009 1 877-859-5095

Price per night: From $105

Description: Enjoy a convenient and comfortable stay at Holiday Inn Express Rotterdam - Central Station, a reliable 3-star hotel ideal for budget-minded travelers. This IHG property offers a familiar standard and a prime location for exploring Rotterdam.

Amenities: Guests can start their day with the hotel's complimentary breakfast buffet, a great way to fuel your adventures. Free Wi-Fi throughout the property keeps you connected. The hotel features soundproofed rooms for a peaceful sleep and offers on-site parking (charges may apply) for those arriving by car.

Nearby Attractions: The hotel's central location next to Rotterdam Central Station provides easy access to the city's public transportation network. Explore the nearby Old Luxor Theater, a historic landmark, or visit the Stadhuis (City Hall), an architectural gem. Take a stroll down the Coolsingel, Rotterdam's main avenue, or visit the Market Hall, a vibrant indoor market.

Why It's Perfect For Travelers:

- **Budget-Friendly Convenience:** Holiday Inn Express offers a reliable and comfortable stay at a competitive price point, perfect for value-conscious travelers.

- **Central Location:** Situated right next to Rotterdam Central Station, you'll enjoy easy access to the city center, public transport, and surrounding areas.

- **Hassle-Free Stay:** Free breakfast, Wi-Fi, and soundproofed rooms ensure a comfortable and convenient stay.

ss Rotterdam

Location: 3e Katendrechtsehoofd 25, 3072 AM Rotterdam The Netherlands

Price per night: NA

Description: Ahoy there! Immerse yourself in maritime history and Rotterdam's rich heritage by staying on the **ss Rotterdam**, a legendary former ocean liner transformed into a unique hotel ship. This grand dame of the Holland-America Line offers a one-of-a-kind experience, seamlessly blending historic charm with modern comforts.

Amenities: Docked in Rotterdam's vibrant Katendrecht district, the ss Rotterdam boasts a variety of amenities to enhance your stay. Explore the meticulously preserved public spaces, including the original first-class dining room and the Captain's Bridge. Several restaurants offer delectable cuisine, while cafes and bars provide opportunities to unwind. For history buffs, guided tours delve into the ship's fascinating past.

Nearby Attractions: Staying on the ss Rotterdam places you right in the heart of the Katendrecht district, known for its trendy bars, street art scene, and industrial warehouses undergoing a cool transformation. Explore the nearby Feyenoord Stadium, home to the legendary Feyenoord football club, or take a scenic ferry ride across the Maas River to Rotterdam's city center.

Why It's Perfect For Travelers:

- **History Buffs:** Sleep in a piece of history and explore the meticulously preserved public areas aboard the ss Rotterdam.

- **Unique Experience:** Enjoy the novelty of staying on a historic ship transformed into a hotel.

- **Foodies and Nightlife Enthusiasts:** Savor delectable cuisine at the ship's restaurants and unwind at the trendy bars in the Katendrecht district.

Rotterdam Marriott Hotel

Location: Weena 686, 3012 CN Rotterdam The Netherlands

Phone: 009 1 844-631-0595

Price per night: NA

Description: Experience sophisticated comfort in the heart of Rotterdam at the Rotterdam Marriott Hotel. This modern 4-star hotel boasts spacious rooms and a central location, ideal for business and leisure travelers alike.

Amenities: Relax in the hotel's M Club Lounge, offering stunning panoramic city views. This exclusive space provides complimentary breakfast, snacks throughout the day, and evening drinks and hors d'oeuvres for members (access may be subject to fees or room type). The hotel also features a well-equipped gym, perfect for staying active. Business travelers can take advantage of the well-appointed meeting rooms and business center.

Nearby Attractions: The Rotterdam Marriott Hotel's prime location directly opposite Rotterdam Central Station allows for effortless exploration of the city. Stroll down the Coolsingel, Rotterdam's main avenue, or visit the nearby Markthal, a vibrant indoor market. Explore the Cube Houses, a unique architectural landmark, or delve into Rotterdam's rich maritime history at the Maritime Museum. Take a scenic boat tour on the historic harbor or enjoy the lively nightlife options in the surrounding area.

Why It's Perfect For Travelers:

- **Central Location:** Situated directly opposite Rotterdam Central Station, you'll enjoy unmatched connectivity to public transportation and easy access to the city center's attractions.

- **Business and Leisure Amenities:** The hotel caters to both business and leisure travelers with well-equipped meeting rooms, a gym, and a relaxing M Club Lounge (access may vary).

- **Comfortable and Sophisticated Stay:** Spacious rooms and modern amenities ensure a comfortable and enjoyable stay in the heart of Rotterdam.

ibis Rotterdam City Centre Hotel

Location: Wijnhaven 12, 3011 WP Rotterdam The Netherlands

Price per night: from $104

Description: Enjoy a comfortable and budget-friendly stay in the heart of Rotterdam at the ibis Rotterdam City Centre Hotel. This modern 3-star hotel offers a convenient location and a focus on functionality, ideal for city explorers.

Amenities: Guests can unwind at the hotel's informal bar with a waterfront terrace, perfect for enjoying a drink and soaking up the city vibes. Free Wi-Fi throughout the property keeps you connected. The hotel prioritizes efficiency with features like 24-hour reception and a cashless payment system.

Nearby Attractions: The ibis Rotterdam City Centre Hotel boasts a prime location in the Wijnhaven harbor district. Explore the nearby Maritime Museum Rotterdam or the Cube Houses, a unique architectural landmark. Take a stroll along the Nieuwe Maas river or visit the Markthal, a stunning indoor market, all within walking distance. The Rotterdam Foodhallen, a vibrant food court, is also just around the corner.

Why It's Perfect For Travelers:

- **Budget-Conscious Travelers:** The ibis Hotel offers a comfortable and affordable stay in a central location, perfect for value-conscious explorers.

- **Convenient Location:** Situated near Blaak Metro stop, you'll enjoy easy access to public transportation and major attractions.

- **Efficient Stay:** Free Wi-Fi, 24-hour reception, and a cashless system ensure a hassle-free and convenient experience.

Family-Friendly Hotels in Rotterdam

Rotterdam, with its modern architecture and vibrant energy, offers a unique city break for families. Here are 5 hotels catering to families, with a range of budgets and locations:

1. MaasHotel Rotterdam Centre:

- **Location:** City Center (Blaak Area)

- **Price:** $100-$150 USD per night

- **Description:** This centrally located hotel offers comfortable accommodations and a good value for budget-conscious families. Family rooms provide extra space, and an indoor pool keeps kids entertained.

- **Nearby Attractions:** Markthal (indoor market), Cube Houses, Maritime Museum, Verkniestraat Playground (walking distance). Excellent public transport connections to other areas.

2. Novotel Rotterdam Brainpark:

- **Location:** Brainpark Area (outside city center)

- **Price:** $120-$180 USD per night

- **Description:** This modern hotel offers spacious, recently renovated rooms, perfect for families. Kids under 16 enjoy complimentary breakfast with their parents. An indoor pool provides entertainment, and the hotel boasts a quieter location with easy access to the city center via a 10-minute metro ride.

- **Nearby Attractions:** Plaswijckpark (green space, petting zoo, mini-golf), Blijdorp Zoo (day trip),

Kinderdijk windmills (day trip). Metro station nearby for easy access to city center attractions.

3. Room Mate Bruno:

- **Location:** Feijenoord District

- **Price:** $150-$200 USD per night

- **Description:** This stylish hotel housed in a historic building offers a unique experience for families with older children. Family rooms provide extra space, and the central location allows for easy exploration. A sauna and steam room offer relaxation for parents after a day of sightseeing.

- **Nearby Attractions:** Fenix Food Factory (vibrant food hall), SS Rotterdam (historic ocean liner turned museum), Erasmus Bridge, Maritime Museum (walking distance). Excellent public transport connections to other areas.

4. Bilderberg Parkhotel Rotterdam:

- **Location:** City Center (Old Town)

- **Price:** $180-$250 USD per night

- **Description:** This comfortable hotel welcomes families and offers amenities like children's beds and cribs (for a surcharge). The central location allows for easy exploration on foot or via public transportation. A breakfast buffet fuels everyone up for a day of adventures.

- **Nearby Attractions:** Markthal, Cube Houses, Witte de Withstraat (shopping street), Kralingse Plas Park (walking distance). Excellent public transport connections to other areas.

5. Van der Valk Hotel Rotterdam-Blijdorp:

- **Location:** Blijdorp Area (outskirts of city)

- **Price:** $130-$200 USD per night (depending on room type)

- **Description:** This upscale hotel offers refined rooms and suites, perfect for families seeking a bit more space. An on-site restaurant caters to all tastes, and room service provides convenience. The hotel offers a free airport shuttle, making arrival and departure a breeze. While outside the city center, it boasts a quiet location near the Blijdorp Zoo.

- **Nearby Attractions:** Blijdorp Zoo (right next door!), Ommoord (shopping center), Plaswijckpark (green space, petting zoo, mini-golf). A taxi or car is recommended for exploring the city center, although public transport options are available.

These are just a few of the many family-friendly hotels Rotterdam has to offer. Remember to consider your budget, desired location, and the age of your children when making your choice. With so much to see and do in this dynamic city, your family is sure to have a memorable Rotterdam vacation!

Budget-Friendly Hotels in Rotterdam: Exploring the City Without Breaking the Bank

Rotterdam offers a vibrant experience for budget-conscious travelers, and families are no exception. Here are 5 hotels that cater to value-seeking guests, with all the essentials for a comfortable stay:

1. easyHotel Rotterdam City Centre:

- **Location:** City Center (Westblaak Area)

- **Price:** $50-$80 USD per night

- **Description:** This no-frills hotel offers compact, clean rooms perfect for budget-minded travelers who prioritize location. Free Wi-Fi keeps everyone connected, and the central location allows for easy exploration of the city on foot or via public transport.

- **Nearby Attractions:** Markthal (indoor market), Cube Houses, Maritime Museum, Witte de Withstraat (shopping street) (walking distance). Excellent public transport connections to other areas.

2. Stayokay Rotterdam - Hostel:

- **Location:** Overblaak Area (near city center)

- **Price:** $60-$100 USD per night (depending on room type)

- **Description:** This lively hostel offers dorm rooms and private rooms at affordable prices. Family rooms provide an option for those seeking more privacy. A communal kitchen allows for preparing meals on a budget, and social events connect you with fellow travelers.

- **Nearby Attractions:** Erasmus Bridge, Witte de Withstraat (shopping street), Kunsthal (contemporary art museum), Het Park (park with boat rentals) (walking distance). Excellent public transport connections to other areas.

3. The Student Hotel Rotterdam:

- **Location:** City Center (Cool District)

- **Price:** $80-$120 USD per night

- **Description:** This trendy hotel caters to a young crowd but offers comfortable rooms at reasonable prices. Family rooms provide an option for families. On-site laundry facilities are a plus for longer stays. A lively atmosphere and social events create a vibrant vibe.

- **Nearby Attractions:** Fenix Food Factory (vibrant food hall), Witte de Withstraat (shopping street), Kunsthal (contemporary art museum), Het Park (park with boat rentals) (walking distance). Excellent public transport connections to other areas.

4. King Kong Hostel:

- **Location:** Witte de Withstraat Area (trendy district)

- **Price:** $40-$70 USD per night (depending on room type)

- **Description:** This funky hostel offers dorm rooms and private rooms at budget-friendly prices. Family rooms provide an option for those seeking more privacy. A communal kitchen allows for preparing meals on a budget, and a bar with events creates a social atmosphere.

- **Nearby Attractions:** Kunsthal (contemporary art museum), Het Park (park with boat rentals), De Markthal (indoor market), Cube Houses (walking distance). Excellent public transport connections to other areas.

5. Ibis Budget Rotterdam The Hague Airport:

- **Location:** Rotterdam Airport Area (outside city center)

- **Price:** $60-$90 USD per night

- **Description:** This conveniently located hotel near the airport offers a good value for budget-conscious travelers, especially those arriving or departing by plane. While outside the city center, a free shuttle service to the airport and good public transport connections make exploring Rotterdam easy. Family rooms provide an option for families.

- **Nearby Attractions:** Rotterdam The Hague Airport (easy access for flights), Plaswijckpark (green space, petting zoo, mini-golf) (short taxi ride), Blijdorp Zoo (day trip). Public transport connections to the city center are available.

Remember, these are just a starting point! Research online for deals and special offers. Many budget hotels offer free breakfast or Wi-Fi, making your stay even more economical. With some planning, you and your family can have a fantastic Rotterdam adventure without breaking the bank!

Vacation Rentals

Rotterdam offers a vibrant mix of modern architecture and historical charm, perfect for exploring as a family or group. Here are some vacation rentals catering to different needs and budgets:

1. Chic Loft Apartment in the Cool District (€€€):

- **Location:** City Center (Cool District)

- **Price:** $200-$300 USD per night

- **Description:** This stylish loft apartment offers a spacious and modern living area, perfect for families or groups. Located in the trendy Cool District, it boasts exposed brick walls, high ceilings, and large windows for an airy feel. A fully equipped kitchen allows for preparing meals, and multiple bedrooms provide privacy.

- **Nearby Attractions:** Fenix Food Factory (vibrant food hall), Witte de Withstraat (shopping street), Kunsthal (contemporary art museum), Het Park (park with boat rentals) (walking distance). Excellent public transport connections to other areas.

2. Cozy Canal Houseboat (Witte de Withstraat Area) (€€):

- **Location:** Witte de Withstraat Area (trendy district)

- **Price:** $150-$250 USD per night

- **Description:** This unique houseboat provides a charming and authentic Rotterdam experience. Located on a quiet canal near the Witte de Withstraat, it offers a comfortable living space with a touch of nautical flair. A small balcony allows for relaxing evenings enjoying the canal views.

- **Nearby Attractions:** Kunsthal (contemporary art museum), Het Park (park with boat rentals), De Markthal (indoor market), Cube Houses (walking distance). Excellent public transport connections to other areas.

3. Family-Friendly Apartment near Euromast (€):

- **Location:** Near Zuidplein (Euromast area)

- **Price:** $100-$180 USD per night

- **Description:** This spacious apartment provides a comfortable and affordable option for families. Located in a quiet residential area near the iconic Euromast observation tower, it offers multiple bedrooms, a fully equipped kitchen, and a living room for relaxing evenings.

- **Nearby Attractions:** Euromast (observation tower with panoramic views), Zuidplein shopping center, Ahoy Rotterdam (events venue), Plaswijckpark (green space, petting zoo, mini-golf) (short taxi ride). Public transport connections to the city center are available.

4. **Modern Studio in the Old Town (€):**

- **Location:** Old Town

- **Price:** $80-$120 USD per night

- **Description:** This modern studio apartment offers a convenient and affordable base for exploring Rotterdam. Located in the historic Old Town, it features a compact living space with a comfortable sleeping area, kitchenette, and a stylish bathroom.

- **Nearby Attractions:** Sint Laurenskerk (St. Lawrence Church), Maritime Museum Rotterdam, De Markthal (indoor market), Cube Houses (walking distance). Excellent public transport connections to other areas.

5. Luxury Apartment with Rooftop Terrace (Scheepvaartkwartier) (€€€):

- **Location:** Scheepvaartkwartier (Historic Harbor District)

- **Price:** $250-$400 USD per night

- **Description:** This luxurious apartment offers stunning views and a touch of opulence. Located in the historic Scheepvaartkwartier, it boasts a spacious living area, modern amenities, and a private rooftop terrace perfect for enjoying panoramic city views.

- **Nearby Attractions:** Historic harbor area, Witte de Withstraat (shopping street), Het Park (park with boat rentals), Maritime Museum Rotterdam (walking distance). Excellent public transport connections to other areas.

Symbol Key:

- € - Budget-Friendly

- €€ - Moderate Price Range

- €€€ - Luxury

Tips:

- Consider the size of your group and desired location when choosing a vacation rental.

- Research amenities like laundry facilities, Wi-Fi, and parking availability.

- Booking platforms often offer deals and discounts, so compare prices before booking.

- Read reviews from previous guests to get insights into the property and the neighborhood.

With a variety of vacation rentals available, Rotterdam can cater to all budgets and travel styles. So pack your bags, book your rental, and get ready to experience the unique charm of this dynamic Dutch city!

CHAPTER THREE

Top Attractions in Rotterdam

Markthal (Market Hall)

Location: Dominee Jan Scharpstraat 298, 3011 GZ Rotterdam

Description: The Markthal, or Market Hall, is a spectacular combination of food market, residential apartments, and commercial space housed within a horseshoe-shaped building. Its striking architecture features a vast arched ceiling adorned with colorful

artwork, making it a feast for the eyes as well as the stomach. Inside, you'll find a bustling market offering a wide array of fresh produce, gourmet delights, and international cuisine. From Dutch cheeses to exotic spices, there's something to tantalize every palate. Don't forget to look up and admire the vibrant ceiling artwork titled "Horn of Plenty," a stunning mural showcasing an abundance of fruits, vegetables, and flowers.

Opening Hours:

- Monday to Saturday: 10:00 AM to 8:00 PM
- Sunday: 12:00 PM to 6:00 PM

Tips for Visitors:

1. **Sampling Local Delicacies:** Take the opportunity to sample traditional Dutch treats like stroopwafels (syrup waffles), bitterballen (deep-fried meatballs), and freshly caught herring from the market stalls.

2. **Photography:** The Markthal's unique architecture and vibrant interior make it a photographer's paradise. Be sure to capture the colorful displays and intricate details throughout the market.

3. **Exploring Surrounding Area:** After visiting the Markthal, take a stroll around the surrounding area of Blaak and admire other architectural wonders such as the Cube Houses and the iconic Erasmus Bridge.

4. **Join a Guided Tour:** For a deeper understanding of the Markthal's history, architecture, and culinary offerings, consider joining a guided tour led by knowledgeable locals who can provide insider insights and recommendations.

5. **Visit During Off-Peak Hours:** To avoid crowds and long lines, consider visiting the Markthal during weekdays or earlier in the morning on weekends.

6. **Accessibility:** The Markthal is wheelchair accessible, with elevators and ramps provided for easy navigation throughout the building.

The Markthal is not just a place to shop for groceries; it's an immersive cultural experience that showcases the diverse flavors and vibrant spirit of Rotterdam. Whether you're a food enthusiast, art lover, or simply curious traveler, a visit to the Markthal promises a memorable taste of Rotterdam's culinary and cultural scene.

Cube Houses (Kijk-Kubus)

Location: Overblaak 70, 3011 MH Rotterdam

Description: Designed by architect Piet Blom in the 1970s, the Cube Houses, or "Kubuswoningen," are a striking example of Rotterdam's avant-garde architecture. These innovative residential units are tilted at a 45-degree angle and are elevated above the ground on hexagonal pylons, resembling a cluster of abstract cubes. The Cube Houses were envisioned as a solution to maximize space in urban environments while offering a unique living experience. While most of the Cube Houses are private residences, one unit has been opened to the public as a museum, allowing visitors to step inside and experience the unconventional design firsthand.

Guided Tours: Guided tours of the Cube Houses are available through the Kijk-Kubus Museum. Knowledgeable guides provide insights into the history, architecture, and concept behind these iconic structures, offering visitors a deeper appreciation of their significance to Rotterdam's architectural landscape.

Opening Hours (Kijk-Kubus Museum):

- Monday to Saturday: 11:00 AM to 5:00 PM
- Sunday: 12:00 PM to 5:00 PM

Tips for Visitors:

1. **Museum Visit:** Start your exploration of the Cube Houses by visiting the Kijk-Kubus Museum, where you can learn about their design principles, construction, and the lifestyle of their inhabitants.

2. **Photography:** The Cube Houses offer endless opportunities for unique and creative photography, with their unconventional angles and geometric shapes. Capture the striking architecture from

different perspectives as you explore the exterior and interior of the museum unit.

3. **Interior Exploration:** While the exterior of the Cube Houses is undoubtedly eye-catching, don't miss the chance to step inside one of the units and experience the clever use of space and light. The museum unit is furnished to showcase how residents adapt to living in these unconventional spaces.

4. **Mind Your Head:** Be mindful of low ceilings and angled walls as you navigate through the Cube Houses, especially if you're tall or have mobility challenges.

5. **Gift Shop:** Don't forget to visit the museum's gift shop, where you can purchase souvenirs and unique gifts inspired by the Cube Houses and Rotterdam's architecture.

Visiting the Cube Houses is not only an opportunity to admire their innovative design but also to gain insights into Rotterdam's reputation as a hub of architectural experimentation and creativity. Whether you're an architecture enthusiast, history buff, or curious traveler, a visit to the Cube Houses promises a memorable and thought-provoking experience.

Erasmus Bridge (Erasmusbrug)

Location: Erasmusbrug, 3072 Rotterdam

Description: Spanning the majestic River Maas, the Erasmus Bridge, or "Erasmusbrug," is an iconic symbol of Rotterdam's modern skyline. Designed by renowned architect Ben van Berkel, this sleek and elegant bridge connects the northern and southern parts of the city, serving as a vital transportation link for pedestrians, cyclists, and motorists. With its distinctive asymmetrical pylon and graceful cable-stayed design, the Erasmus

Bridge is not only a feat of engineering but also a striking piece of contemporary architecture that has become synonymous with Rotterdam's identity.

Highlights:

1. **Panoramic Views:** Walk or cycle across the Erasmus Bridge and soak in breathtaking panoramic views of Rotterdam's waterfront, skyline, and bustling port. The bridge offers unparalleled vistas, particularly during sunrise or sunset when the city is bathed in golden light.

2. **Photography:** Capture the beauty of the Erasmus Bridge from various vantage points along the riverbank or from neighboring landmarks such as the Kop van Zuid district. Experiment with different angles and perspectives to showcase the bridge's architectural elegance and the dynamic cityscape.

3. **Maasboulevard:** After crossing the bridge, explore the vibrant Maasboulevard promenade, lined with cafes, restaurants, and recreational facilities. Take a leisurely stroll along the waterfront or relax on one of the benches while

enjoying views of passing ships and waterfront activities.

4. **Night Illumination:** Experience the Erasmus Bridge in all its illuminated glory after dark when it is bathed in colorful LED lights. The bridge's lighting scheme adds a captivating element to Rotterdam's nighttime skyline, creating a mesmerizing spectacle that shouldn't be missed.

5. **Landmark Landmark:** The Erasmus Bridge serves as a landmark and meeting point for locals and visitors alike. Whether you're meeting friends for a picnic in the nearby parks or attending events and festivals along the riverfront, the bridge provides a central focal point for navigation and orientation in the city.

Practical Tips:

1. **Accessibility:** The Erasmus Bridge is accessible to pedestrians, cyclists, and motorists. If walking or cycling, be mindful of other users and follow designated pathways and crossings.

2. **Public Transportation:** The bridge is easily accessible via public transportation, with tram and

bus stops located nearby. Consider using Rotterdam's efficient public transit system to reach the bridge and explore the surrounding area.

3. **Weather Conditions:** Be prepared for windy conditions when crossing the Erasmus Bridge, especially during inclement weather. Dress accordingly and bring along a jacket or sweater to stay comfortable, particularly if visiting during colder months.

4. **Safety Precautions:** Exercise caution when taking photographs or admiring the views from the bridge, especially if leaning over railings or standing near traffic. Stay aware of your surroundings and adhere to safety guidelines to ensure a safe and enjoyable experience.

The Erasmus Bridge is more than just a crossing; it's a symbol of Rotterdam's resilience, innovation, and forward-thinking spirit. Whether you're marveling at its architectural beauty, enjoying panoramic views of the city, or simply crossing from one side to the other, the Erasmus Bridge offers a memorable and immersive experience that encapsulates the essence of Rotterdam's dynamic urban landscape.

The Rotterdam (formerly SS Rotterdam)

Location: 3e Katendrechtse Hoofd 25, 3072 AM Rotterdam

Description: The Rotterdam, also known as the SS Rotterdam, is a historic ocean liner that has been lovingly restored and repurposed as a multi-functional attraction in Rotterdam. Built in the 1950s for the Holland America Line, the Rotterdam was once a glamorous mode of transatlantic travel, ferrying passengers between Europe and North America. Today, it stands proudly as a floating museum, hotel, event venue, and dining destination, offering visitors a glimpse into the golden age of ocean travel.

Highlights:

1. **Ship Tours:** Explore the decks of the Rotterdam on guided tours that take you through its storied history and iconic features. From the elegant ballrooms and luxurious cabins to the engine room and bridge, discover the inner workings of this magnificent vessel and learn about its role in maritime history.

2. **Museum Exhibits:** Immerse yourself in the maritime heritage of the Rotterdam through interactive exhibits, artifacts, and archival photographs displayed throughout the ship. Gain insight into the daily life of passengers and crew members, as well as the technological innovations that propelled the vessel across the seas.

3. **Hotel Accommodations:** Experience a unique stay aboard the Rotterdam by booking a room in one of its well-appointed cabins. Whether you opt for a cozy interior cabin or a spacious suite with panoramic views of the river, enjoy modern amenities combined with nostalgic touches that evoke the glamour of ocean liner travel.

4. **Dining and Entertainment:** Indulge in culinary delights at one of the Rotterdam's onboard restaurants, which offer a diverse range of cuisine inspired by the ship's international voyages. From fine dining to casual fare, savor delectable dishes while enjoying panoramic views of the river and city skyline. Additionally, the Rotterdam hosts regular events, including live music performances, themed parties, and cultural celebrations.

5. **Event Venue:** Host your next event or celebration in one of the Rotterdam's elegant event spaces, which can accommodate weddings, conferences, corporate functions, and private gatherings. Whether you're planning a lavish banquet in the Grand Ballroom or a cocktail reception on the Promenade Deck, the Rotterdam provides a unique and memorable setting for any occasion.

Practical Tips:

1. **Booking Reservations:** Advance reservations are recommended for ship tours, hotel accommodations, and dining experiences aboard the Rotterdam, especially during peak tourist seasons and special events.

2. **Accessibility:** While efforts have been made to make the Rotterdam accessible to visitors with mobility impairments, please check with staff for specific accommodations and accessibility features prior to your visit.

3. **Parking and Transportation:** The Rotterdam offers parking facilities for guests arriving by car, as well as convenient access to public transportation options, including tram and bus stops nearby.

4. **Photography:** Capture memories of your visit aboard the Rotterdam, but be mindful of any photography restrictions in certain areas of the ship, especially those containing sensitive historical artifacts.

5. **Gift Shop:** Browse the onboard gift shop for souvenirs, maritime-themed gifts, and memorabilia to commemorate your visit to the Rotterdam.

The Rotterdam offers a unique blend of history, luxury, and entertainment, making it a must-visit destination for maritime enthusiasts, history buffs, and curious travelers alike. Whether you're exploring its museum exhibits, enjoying a gourmet meal, or simply soaking in the nostalgic ambiance of this iconic ocean liner, a visit to the Rotterdam promises an unforgettable experience on the waters of Rotterdam.

De Rotterdam (Skyscraper)

Location: Wilhelminakade 143, 3072 AP Rotterdam

Description: De Rotterdam is a stunning architectural masterpiece and one of the most prominent landmarks in Rotterdam's skyline. Designed by renowned architect Rem

Koolhaas and his firm, OMA, this striking skyscraper complex is a symbol of Rotterdam's modernity and innovation. Completed in 2013, De Rotterdam consists of three interconnected towers rising to a height of 150 meters, with a total floor area of approximately 160,000 square meters. The towers are characterized by their sleek, minimalist design and staggered arrangement, creating a dynamic and visually captivating profile that stands out against the cityscape.

Highlights:

1. **Architecture:** Admire the bold and futuristic design of De Rotterdam, characterized by its clean lines, reflective glass facades, and distinctive massing. Marvel at the interplay of light and shadow as the towers soar skyward, creating a dramatic presence on the waterfront.

2. **Observation Deck:** Enjoy panoramic views of Rotterdam and the surrounding area from the observation deck located on the upper floors of De Rotterdam. Take in sweeping vistas of the River Maas, Erasmus Bridge, and iconic landmarks such as the Euromast and Markthal, providing a unique perspective on the city's urban fabric.

3. **Mixed-Use Complex:** Experience the vibrant energy of De Rotterdam's mixed-use program, which includes office spaces, residential apartments, hotel accommodations, retail outlets, and dining establishments. Discover a diverse array of amenities and services conveniently located within the complex, catering to both residents and visitors alike.

4. **Public Spaces:** Explore the public spaces within De Rotterdam, including atriums, plazas, and landscaped areas that serve as gathering spaces for tenants and the surrounding community. Admire the integration of art and design elements throughout the complex, enhancing the overall aesthetic and user experience.

5. **Cultural Events:** Attend cultural events, exhibitions, and performances hosted within De Rotterdam's multifunctional spaces, which serve as venues for art, music, film, and other creative endeavors. Immerse yourself in Rotterdam's vibrant cultural scene while enjoying the contemporary ambiance of this iconic landmark.

Practical Tips:

1. **Visiting Hours:** Check the opening hours of specific attractions and amenities within De Rotterdam, such as the observation deck, restaurants, and retail establishments, as they may vary depending on the day and time.

2. **Ticketing:** Purchase tickets in advance for access to the observation deck or other attractions within De Rotterdam, especially during peak tourist seasons and holidays.

3. **Accessibility:** De Rotterdam is wheelchair accessible, with designated entrances, elevators, and facilities to accommodate visitors with mobility impairments. If you have specific accessibility needs, contact the venue in advance for assistance.

4. **Photography:** Capture memorable moments and stunning views of Rotterdam from De Rotterdam's observation deck and public spaces. Remember to respect privacy and property rights when taking photographs, especially in residential areas.

5. **Transportation:** Reach De Rotterdam easily by public transportation, including tram, metro, and

water taxi services, as well as by car or bicycle. Plan your route in advance and check for parking facilities or bike racks near the complex.

De Rotterdam stands as a testament to Rotterdam's commitment to architectural excellence, urban innovation, and sustainable development. Whether you're admiring its sleek design from afar or exploring its vibrant interior spaces up close, a visit to De Rotterdam offers a captivating journey through the dynamic spirit of Rotterdam's waterfront district.

Delfshaven

Location: Delfshaven, Rotterdam, Netherlands

Description: Delfshaven is a picturesque and historic neighborhood situated within the city of Rotterdam. Unlike much of Rotterdam, Delfshaven largely survived the bombings of World War II, allowing its charming 17th-century architecture and maritime heritage to remain intact. The neighborhood is characterized by its quaint canals, cobblestone streets, and preserved buildings, offering visitors a glimpse into Rotterdam's rich maritime history and cultural heritage.

Highlights:

1. **Historic Harbor:** Explore the historic harbor of Delfshaven, which was once a bustling center of maritime trade and commerce. Admire the traditional Dutch ships moored along the quaysides, and soak in the maritime ambiance of this centuries-old port.

2. **Delfshaven Church:** Visit the Delfshaven Church (Oude Kerk), a historic landmark dating back to the 15th century. This Gothic-style church features a distinctive tower and interior furnishings, including stained glass windows and ornate wooden pews. Climb the tower for panoramic views of Delfshaven and the surrounding area.

3. **Pilgrim Fathers' Church:** Discover the Pilgrim Fathers' Church (Pelgrimvaderskerk), where a group of English Pilgrims worshipped before embarking on their journey to the New World aboard the Mayflower in 1620. Learn about the history of the Pilgrims and their connection to Delfshaven through exhibitions and guided tours.

4. **Historic Buildings:** Wander through Delfshaven's narrow streets and alleyways lined

with well-preserved historic buildings, including merchant houses, warehouses, and breweries. Admire the distinctive Dutch architecture adorned with gabled facades, stepped roofs, and ornate facades, reflecting the neighborhood's prosperous past.

5. **Museums and Galleries:** Immerse yourself in Delfshaven's cultural scene by visiting local museums and galleries showcasing art, history, and maritime heritage. Explore exhibits on topics such as Dutch colonial history, maritime trade, and the life and times of Delfshaven's inhabitants through the centuries.

Practical Tips:

1. **Walking Tour:** Take a self-guided walking tour of Delfshaven to explore its historic landmarks and hidden gems at your own pace. Pick up a map or guidebook from the tourist information center or download a digital guide to help navigate the neighborhood's winding streets.

2. **Canal Cruise:** Experience Delfshaven from a different perspective by taking a canal cruise along its tranquil waterways. Relax onboard a traditional

Dutch boat as you glide past historic buildings, bridges, and waterfront attractions, while learning about the neighborhood's history from knowledgeable guides.

3. **Cafes and Restaurants:** Enjoy a meal or drink at one of Delfshaven's charming cafes, restaurants, or waterfront terraces. Sample local specialties such as herring, Dutch pancakes, or craft beers while soaking in the scenic views of the harbor and surrounding architecture.

4. **Shopping:** Browse boutique shops, antique stores, and artisanal markets in Delfshaven to find unique souvenirs, gifts, and handmade crafts. Support local artisans and businesses while discovering treasures ranging from vintage clothing to handmade ceramics.

5. **Events and Festivals:** Check local event calendars for festivals, markets, and cultural events taking place in Delfshaven throughout the year. Experience traditional Dutch celebrations, live music performances, and cultural festivities that showcase the vibrant spirit of the neighborhood.

Delfshaven offers a delightful blend of history, culture, and charm, making it a must-visit destination for travelers seeking an authentic experience in Rotterdam. Whether you're exploring its historic landmarks, dining at waterfront cafes, or simply strolling along its picturesque canals, Delfshaven invites you to step back in time and discover the timeless beauty of Rotterdam's maritime heritage.

Sint Laurenskerk (St. Lawrence Church)

Location: Grotekerkplein 27, 3011 GC Rotterdam

Description: Sint Laurenskerk, also known as St. Lawrence Church, is a magnificent Gothic-style church located in the heart of Rotterdam. Dating back to the 15th century, this historic landmark is one of the few buildings in Rotterdam to have survived the bombings of World War II, making it a symbol of resilience and endurance for the city. With its soaring spire, intricate stonework, and stunning stained glass windows, Sint Laurenskerk stands as a testament to Rotterdam's rich religious heritage and architectural legacy.

Highlights:

1. **Architectural Marvel:** Marvel at the awe-inspiring architecture of Sint Laurenskerk, characterized by its towering spire, ornate facades, and soaring vaulted ceilings. Admire the intricate details of the Gothic-style stonework, including gargoyles, sculptures, and decorative carvings that adorn the exterior and interior of the church.

2. **Stained Glass Windows:** Step inside Sint Laurenskerk to discover a treasure trove of stained glass windows dating from various periods in history. Admire the vibrant colors, intricate patterns, and biblical scenes depicted in these exquisite works of art, which add warmth and luminosity to the church's interior.

3. **Historical Significance:** Learn about the rich history and cultural significance of Sint Laurenskerk through guided tours, exhibitions, and educational programs offered by the church. Gain insight into the church's role in Rotterdam's religious and civic life over the centuries, as well as its enduring legacy as a symbol of hope and renewal.

4. **Organ Concerts:** Experience the majestic sound of the church's historic organ during organ concerts held throughout the year. Listen to talented musicians perform classical compositions, sacred music, and improvisations that showcase the instrument's rich tones and capabilities in the acoustically impressive space of Sint Laurenskerk.

5. **Cultural Events:** Attend cultural events, lectures, and performances hosted within Sint Laurenskerk, which serves as a vibrant hub for artistic and community activities. From classical music concerts to art exhibitions and poetry readings, the church offers a diverse range of cultural experiences that appeal to visitors of all ages and interests.

Practical Tips:

1. **Visiting Hours:** Check the opening hours of Sint Laurenskerk for guided tours, worship services, and special events, as they may vary depending on the day and time.

2. **Photography:** Capture the beauty and grandeur of Sint Laurenskerk through photography, but be respectful of any guidelines or restrictions

regarding photography during religious services or private events.

3. **Dress Code:** Dress modestly when visiting Sint Laurenskerk out of respect for its religious significance. Avoid wearing revealing clothing or attire that may be considered inappropriate for a place of worship.

4. **Donations:** Consider making a voluntary donation to support the ongoing maintenance and preservation efforts of Sint Laurenskerk, ensuring that future generations can continue to appreciate its architectural and cultural heritage.

5. **Accessibility:** Sint Laurenskerk is wheelchair accessible, with ramps and designated entrances provided for visitors with mobility impairments. If you have specific accessibility needs, contact the church in advance for assistance.

Sint Laurenskerk is not just a place of worship; it's a living testament to Rotterdam's history, heritage, and enduring spirit. Whether you're admiring its architectural splendor, attending a cultural event, or simply seeking solace in its sacred space, a visit to Sint Laurenskerk offers a profound and enriching experience that resonates with visitors long after they've left its hallowed halls.

Maritime Museum Rotterdam

Location: Leuvehaven 1, 3011 EA Rotterdam

Description: The Maritime Museum Rotterdam offers an immersive journey into the rich maritime history and culture of Rotterdam and the Netherlands. Housed within a historic warehouse complex in the bustling Leuvehaven harbor area, the museum showcases a diverse range of exhibits, artifacts, and interactive displays that bring the seafaring heritage of Rotterdam to life. From ancient seafaring traditions to modern shipping technology, the Maritime Museum offers something for visitors of all ages to explore and discover.

Highlights:

1. **Main Exhibition:** Explore the main exhibition halls of the Maritime Museum to uncover the fascinating story of Rotterdam's maritime past and present. Learn about the city's evolution from a modest fishing village to one of the world's largest

and busiest ports through interactive displays, historical artifacts, and multimedia presentations.

2. **Ship Models:** Admire an extensive collection of ship models representing various types of vessels, from ancient sailing ships to modern cargo carriers and naval vessels. Marvel at the craftsmanship and attention to detail in these intricate scale replicas, which offer insights into the design, construction, and operation of ships throughout history.

3. **Historic Ships:** Step aboard historic ships moored in the harbor adjacent to the museum, including the iconic steam-powered tugboat "Dockyard V," the last surviving steam tug of its kind in the Netherlands. Explore the decks, cabins, and engine rooms of these venerable vessels and imagine life at sea during different eras of maritime history.

4. **Interactive Exhibits:** Engage with interactive exhibits and hands-on activities that provide a deeper understanding of maritime concepts, navigation techniques, and marine ecosystems. Test your skills as a ship captain, navigate virtual sailing simulations, and learn about the importance

of conservation and sustainability in modern maritime industries.

5. **Special Exhibitions:** Discover rotating special exhibitions that delve into specific aspects of maritime history, culture, and innovation. From temporary displays highlighting famous shipwrecks and maritime disasters to exhibitions showcasing contemporary maritime art and design, there's always something new and exciting to see at the Maritime Museum.

Practical Tips:

1. **Opening Hours:** Check the museum's website for current opening hours and special events, as they may vary depending on the season and exhibition schedule.

2. **Guided Tours:** Consider joining a guided tour of the museum led by knowledgeable staff or volunteers who can provide insights into the exhibits and answer questions about Rotterdam's maritime heritage.

3. **Visitor Amenities:** Take advantage of visitor amenities such as cafes, gift shops, and rest areas

located within the museum complex. Refuel with refreshments, browse maritime-themed souvenirs, and relax in comfortable seating areas between exhibitions.

4. **Accessibility:** The Maritime Museum is wheelchair accessible, with ramps, elevators, and designated parking spaces available for visitors with mobility impairments. If you have specific accessibility needs, contact the museum in advance for assistance.

5. **Combination Tickets:** Save money by purchasing combination tickets that grant access to multiple attractions in Rotterdam, including the Maritime Museum and other cultural institutions and landmarks in the city.

The Maritime Museum Rotterdam offers a captivating blend of history, innovation, and exploration that appeals to maritime enthusiasts, history buffs, and curious travelers alike. Whether you're delving into the past through interactive exhibits, exploring historic ships, or admiring intricate ship models, a visit to the Maritime Museum promises an unforgettable voyage of discovery through the maritime heritage of Rotterdam and the Netherlands.

Kunsthal Rotterdam

Location: Westzeedijk 341, 3015 AA Rotterdam

Description: The Kunsthal Rotterdam is a dynamic cultural institution dedicated to showcasing a diverse range of art, design, and cultural exhibitions from around the world. Designed by the renowned architect Rem Koolhaas, the Kunsthal's distinctive architecture provides a striking backdrop for its ever-changing roster of temporary exhibitions, which span various genres, styles, and time periods. From contemporary art and photography to fashion, design, and multimedia installations, the Kunsthal offers a thought-provoking and immersive experience for visitors of all ages and interests.

Highlights:

1. **Exhibition Spaces:** Explore the Kunsthal's spacious exhibition halls, which host a rotating schedule of temporary exhibitions throughout the year. From blockbuster shows featuring works by internationally acclaimed artists to niche

exhibitions highlighting emerging talents and innovative trends, there's always something new and exciting to discover at the Kunsthal.

2. **Contemporary Art:** Immerse yourself in the vibrant world of contemporary art through thought-provoking exhibitions that challenge conventions, inspire dialogue, and push the boundaries of artistic expression. Experience a diverse range of media, techniques, and conceptual themes as you engage with works by both established and emerging artists from across the globe.

3. **Photography:** Delve into the captivating world of photography through exhibitions that showcase the power of the visual medium to document, interpret, and communicate the human experience. From documentary photography and photojournalism to fine art photography and experimental techniques, the Kunsthal offers a rich and diverse selection of photographic works that resonate with viewers on both intellectual and emotional levels.

4. **Design and Fashion:** Discover the intersection of art, design, and fashion through exhibitions that

explore the creative process, innovation, and cultural significance of these interconnected disciplines. From avant-garde fashion collections and architectural installations to product design and digital media, the Kunsthal celebrates the diversity and dynamism of contemporary design practices.

5. **Educational Programs:** Engage with educational programs, workshops, and guided tours offered by the Kunsthal to deepen your understanding of art, culture, and creativity. Learn from experts, artists, and curators who provide insights, context, and interpretation for the exhibitions on display, fostering a deeper appreciation and connection to the artwork.

Practical Tips:

1. **Opening Hours:** Check the Kunsthal's website for current opening hours, exhibition schedules, and ticket information, as they may vary depending on the season and specific exhibitions.

2. **Accessibility:** The Kunsthal is wheelchair accessible, with ramps, elevators, and designated parking spaces available for visitors with mobility

impairments. If you have specific accessibility needs, contact the Kunsthal in advance for assistance.

3. **Visitor Amenities:** Take advantage of visitor amenities such as cafes, gift shops, and rest areas located within the Kunsthal. Grab a coffee, browse art books and merchandise, and relax in comfortable seating areas before or after exploring the exhibitions.

4. **Photography Policy:** Respect the Kunsthal's photography policy, which may vary depending on the specific exhibition and artist's copyright restrictions. Avoid using flash photography or tripods unless explicitly permitted, and be mindful of any signage or guidelines regarding photography within the exhibition spaces.

5. **Public Transportation:** Reach the Kunsthal easily by public transportation, including tram, bus, and metro services, as well as by car or bicycle. Plan your route in advance and check for parking facilities or bike racks near the Kunsthal.

The Kunsthal Rotterdam offers a dynamic and engaging cultural experience that celebrates creativity, diversity, and innovation in the arts. Whether you're exploring cutting-edge contemporary art, immersing yourself in photographic storytelling, or discovering the latest trends in design and fashion, a visit to the Kunsthal promises an enriching and inspiring journey through the world of visual culture.

Museum Boijmans Van Beuningen

Location: Museumpark 18-20, 3015 CX Rotterdam

Description: Museum Boijmans Van Beuningen is one of the oldest museums in the Netherlands, renowned for its extensive collection of fine art, decorative arts, and design spanning from the Middle Ages to the present day. Situated in the heart of Rotterdam's cultural district, the museum's diverse holdings encompass a wide range of artistic genres, including painting, sculpture, prints, drawings, applied arts, and design objects. With works by renowned artists such as Rembrandt, Van Gogh, Monet, and Mondrian, as well as contemporary masters and emerging talents, Museum Boijmans Van Beuningen offers a comprehensive overview of the history of art and visual culture.

Highlights:

1. **Permanent Collection:** Explore the museum's permanent collection, which features masterpieces from various periods and art movements, including Dutch and Flemish Old Masters, Impressionism, Surrealism, and Modernism. Admire iconic works such as Hieronymus Bosch's "The Garden of Earthly Delights," Pieter Bruegel the Elder's "The Tower of Babel," and Salvador Dalí's "The Persistence of Memory," among many others.

2. **Modern and Contemporary Art:** Immerse yourself in the vibrant world of modern and contemporary art through exhibitions that showcase groundbreaking works by 20th and 21st-century artists. Experience innovative approaches to painting, sculpture, installation, and new media as you engage with thought-provoking artworks that challenge conventions and redefine artistic boundaries.

3. **Design Collection:** Discover the museum's extensive collection of applied arts and design objects, which encompasses furniture, ceramics, glassware, textiles, and industrial design from

around the world. From Art Nouveau and Art Deco to Bauhaus and Dutch Design, explore the evolution of design aesthetics and techniques through iconic pieces by renowned designers and craftsmen.

4. **Special Exhibitions:** Experience rotating special exhibitions that highlight specific themes, artists, or art movements, offering fresh perspectives and insights into the museum's collection and the broader landscape of art history. From retrospective surveys to thematic explorations, these exhibitions provide opportunities for deeper engagement and discovery for visitors of all interests.

5. **Educational Programs:** Engage with educational programs, workshops, and guided tours offered by Museum Boijmans Van Beuningen to enhance your understanding and appreciation of art and culture. Learn from knowledgeable curators, educators, and artists who provide context, interpretation, and hands-on experiences that enrich your museum visit.

Practical Tips:

1. **Opening Hours:** Check the museum's website for current opening hours, exhibition schedules, and ticket information, as they may vary depending on the season and specific exhibitions.

2. **Guided Tours:** Consider joining a guided tour of the museum led by knowledgeable staff or volunteers who can provide insights into the artworks, artists, and historical contexts represented in the collection.

3. **Visitor Amenities:** Take advantage of visitor amenities such as cafes, gift shops, and rest areas located within the museum. Refuel with refreshments, browse art books and souvenirs, and relax in comfortable seating areas between gallery visits.

4. **Accessibility:** Museum Boijmans Van Beuningen is wheelchair accessible, with ramps, elevators, and designated parking spaces available for visitors with mobility impairments. If you have specific accessibility needs, contact the museum in advance for assistance.

5. **Public Transportation:** Reach the museum easily by public transportation, including tram, bus, and metro services, as well as by car or bicycle. Plan your route in advance and check for parking facilities or bike racks near the museum.

Museum Boijmans Van Beuningen offers a rich and multifaceted cultural experience that celebrates the diversity and dynamism of art and design. Whether you're exploring masterpieces from centuries past, discovering cutting-edge contemporary art, or immersing yourself in the world of design and decorative arts, a visit to Museum Boijmans Van Beuningen promises an enriching and inspiring journey through the history of human creativity.

Het Park

Location: Westzeedijk, 3016 Rotterdam, Netherlands

Description: Het Park, translated as "The Park," is a serene and expansive green space located in the heart of Rotterdam. Situated adjacent to the Museum Park and overlooking the River Maas, Het Park offers a tranquil retreat from the bustling city center, providing locals and visitors alike with opportunities for relaxation, recreation, and leisurely strolls amidst lush greenery and scenic landscapes. Originally designed in the 19th century by landscape architect Jan David Zocher, Het Park is a beloved urban oasis that embodies Rotterdam's commitment to preserving and enhancing its natural environment for the enjoyment of all.

Highlights:

1. **Scenic Views:** Enjoy panoramic views of the River Maas, Erasmus Bridge, and Rotterdam skyline from various vantage points within Het Park. Capture picturesque scenes of passing ships, waterfront promenades, and iconic landmarks as you meander through the park's winding pathways and open spaces.

2. **Historic Features:** Discover historic monuments, sculptures, and architectural landmarks scattered throughout Het Park, including the Park House (Parkhuys), Park Pavilion (Parkpaviljoen), and the Roman-style Temple of Remembrance (Tempel der Gedachtenis). Learn about the park's rich history and cultural significance through interpretive signage and guided tours.

3. **Botanical Diversity:** Explore Het Park's diverse array of plantings, including mature trees, flowering shrubs, and seasonal blooms that create a vibrant tapestry of colors and textures throughout the year. Take a leisurely stroll through tree-lined avenues, formal gardens, and shaded groves, and immerse yourself in the natural beauty and tranquility of the park's verdant landscapes.

4. **Recreational Activities:** Engage in recreational activities and outdoor pursuits within Het Park, such as picnicking, jogging, cycling, and birdwatching. Unwind with a leisurely picnic on the grassy lawns, embark on a scenic bike ride along designated paths, or simply bask in the sun while admiring the beauty of your surroundings.

5. **Cultural Events:** Attend cultural events, concerts, and festivals held within Het Park throughout the year, which showcase a diverse range of artistic performances, live music, and community celebrations. Experience the vibrant energy and creative spirit of Rotterdam's cultural scene against the backdrop of the park's natural splendor.

Practical Tips:

1. **Opening Hours:** Het Park is open to the public year-round, with varying hours depending on the season and weather conditions. Check local park regulations and signage for specific opening and closing times, as well as any temporary closures or restrictions.

2. **Facilities:** While exploring Het Park, take advantage of visitor amenities such as benches, picnic areas, and public restrooms located throughout the park. Pack essentials such as sunscreen, water, and snacks for a comfortable and enjoyable outdoor experience.

3. **Pet-Friendly:** Het Park welcomes leashed pets, providing a scenic and spacious environment for dogs and their owners to enjoy together. Be respectful of other park users and clean up after your pet to maintain the park's cleanliness and hygiene.

4. **Safety:** Exercise caution and adhere to safety guidelines when engaging in recreational activities or exploring remote areas of Het Park, especially after dark or during inclement weather. Stay on

designated paths, avoid isolated areas, and be mindful of potential hazards such as uneven terrain or wildlife.

5. **Transportation:** Access Het Park easily by public transportation, including tram, bus, and metro services, as well as by car or bicycle. Plan your route in advance and check for parking facilities or bike racks near the park entrance.

Het Park offers a tranquil retreat and scenic escape in the heart of Rotterdam, inviting visitors to reconnect with nature, unwind amidst lush landscapes, and embrace the beauty of urban green spaces. Whether you're seeking solitude and relaxation or socializing with friends and family, Het Park provides a serene and inviting backdrop for memorable outdoor experiences and leisurely moments of contemplation.

Kinderdijk Windmills

Location: Nederwaard 1, 2961 AS Kinderdijk, Netherlands

Description: Kinderdijk is a UNESCO World Heritage site located in the Alblasserwaard region of South

Holland, renowned for its iconic windmills and historic water management system. Dating back to the 18th century, the Kinderdijk windmills were constructed to drain excess water from the low-lying polders and prevent flooding in the surrounding agricultural land. Today, Kinderdijk is home to a picturesque landscape dotted with 19 well-preserved windmills, making it one of the most iconic and recognizable landmarks in the Netherlands.

Highlights:

1. **Windmill Tour:** Embark on a guided tour of the Kinderdijk windmills to learn about their fascinating history, engineering, and cultural significance. Explore the interior of select windmills that have been preserved as museums, providing insights into the daily lives of millers and the mechanics of traditional windmill operation.

2. **Scenic Landscape:** Wander through the scenic landscape of Kinderdijk, which features winding footpaths, cycling trails, and panoramic viewpoints offering breathtaking vistas of the windmills, canals, and surrounding countryside. Capture postcard-perfect photos of the iconic silhouette of

the windmills against the backdrop of open skies and tranquil waters.

3. **Visitor Center:** Visit the Kinderdijk Visitor Center to access informative exhibits, multimedia presentations, and interactive displays that provide context and interpretation for the site's cultural and natural heritage. Learn about the challenges of water management in the Netherlands and the innovative techniques employed by the Dutch to reclaim land from the sea.

4. **Boat Tours:** Experience Kinderdijk from a different perspective by taking a scenic boat tour along the canals that crisscross the landscape. Glide past the windmills, bridges, and historic waterways while enjoying commentary from knowledgeable guides who share insights into the area's history, ecology, and engineering feats.

5. **Cultural Events:** Attend special events, festivals, and cultural programs held at Kinderdijk throughout the year, which showcase traditional Dutch customs, music, dance, and cuisine. Experience the vibrant spirit of local communities

and immerse yourself in the rich cultural heritage of the Alblasserwaard region.

Practical Tips:

1. **Opening Hours:** Check the Kinderdijk website for current opening hours, guided tour schedules, and ticket information, as they may vary depending on the season and weather conditions.

2. **Accessibility:** Kinderdijk is wheelchair accessible, with designated pathways and viewing areas provided for visitors with mobility impairments. Some windmills may have limited accessibility due to narrow staircases and uneven terrain, so check with staff for accessibility options and assistance.

3. **Visitor Facilities:** Take advantage of visitor facilities such as restrooms, cafes, and souvenir shops located near the entrance of Kinderdijk. Purchase tickets, pick up informational brochures, and inquire about guided tours or boat excursions at the visitor center.

4. **Weather Preparedness:** Dress appropriately for the weather conditions when visiting Kinderdijk, especially if exploring outdoor pathways and

exposed areas. Bring layers, rain gear, and sturdy footwear to ensure comfort and protection from the elements.

5. **Transportation:** Access Kinderdijk easily by public transportation, including bus, waterbus, or bicycle, as well as by car. Plan your route in advance and check for parking facilities or bike racks near the entrance of Kinderdijk.

Kinderdijk Windmills offer a captivating blend of natural beauty, cultural heritage, and engineering marvels that appeal to visitors of all ages and interests. Whether you're exploring the windmills on foot, cruising along the canals by boat, or delving into the history of water management at the visitor center, a visit to Kinderdijk promises an unforgettable journey through the quintessential Dutch landscape and centuries-old traditions of windmill technology.

CHAPTER FOUR

Rotterdam Tours to Uncover the City's Hidden Gems and Must-See Sights

1. **Rotterdam Highlights: City & Harbor Tour (Boot10):** Explore Rotterdam by land and water on this comprehensive tour by Boot10.

    - **Location:** City Center (Meeting Point: Boat tours depart from the Erasmus Bridge)

    - **End Point:** Same as Meeting Point

    - **Highlights:** Cruise along the historic harbor, marvel at the Erasmus Bridge, admire the Cube Houses, and delve into Rotterdam's fascinating history and modern architecture with live commentary.

2. **Unseen Rotterdam: Secret Canals Tour (Rotterdam Discovery Tours):** Unveil Rotterdam's hidden waterways on a unique canal tour with Rotterdam Discovery Tours.

- **Location:** City Center (Meeting Point: Specific location provided upon booking)

- **End Point:** Same as Meeting Point (or near Market Hall)

- **Highlights:** Glide through hidden canals, discover historic warehouses, peek into charming courtyards, and learn about Rotterdam's hidden stories and lesser-known landmarks.

3. **Street Art Tour: Urban Canvas Exploration (Rotterdam Street Art Tours):** Immerse yourself in Rotterdam's vibrant street art scene with Rotterdam Street Art Tours.

    - **Location:** Various locations throughout the city (Meeting Point changes based on tour route - details provided upon booking)

    - **End Point:** Varies depending on chosen tour route

    - **Highlights:** Explore hidden alleyways and discover stunning murals by world-renowned street artists. Learn about the history and techniques of street art, and gain insights into Rotterdam's creative spirit.

4. **Culinary Adventure: Rotterdam Food Tour (Feyenoord Tours & Tastings):** Tantalize your taste buds on a delicious food tour with Feyenoord Tours & Tastings.

    - **Location:** Various Locations in Feijenoord District (Meeting Point: Specific location provided upon booking)

    - **End Point:** Near Market Hall

    - **Highlights:** Sample local delicacies, explore hidden gems of the Feijenoord district, visit a traditional Dutch cheese shop, indulge in fresh seafood at a harborside restaurant, and learn about Rotterdam's diverse culinary scene.

5. **Architecture Enthusiast's Dream: Modern Marvels Tour (Rotterdam Architectuur):** Dive deep into Rotterdam's architectural wonders with Rotterdam Architectuur.

    - **Location:** City Center (Meeting Point: Kunsthal Rotterdam)

    - **End Point:** Markthal

- **Highlights:** Explore iconic landmarks like the Cube Houses, Erasmus Bridge, and the Markthal, guided by an architect who will unveil the stories behind these modern marvels. Learn about Rotterdam's innovative and sustainable architecture.

6. **Rotterdam by Night: Illuminated City Tour (Rotterdam Lights):** Witness Rotterdam's magical transformation after dark on a tour with Rotterdam Lights.

    - **Location:** City Center (Meeting Point: De Rotterdam Tours office near Erasmus Bridge)

    - **End Point:** Same as Meeting Point

    - **Highlights:** See Rotterdam's iconic landmarks illuminated against the night sky, enjoy the vibrant nightlife atmosphere, and discover hidden gems with a new perspective.

7. **Family Fun: Rotterdam with Kids Tour (Tours & Kids):** Keep the whole family entertained on a fun-filled tour with Tours & Kids.

- **Location:** City Center (Meeting Point: Varies depending on chosen tour - details provided upon booking)

- **End Point:** Varies depending on chosen tour - may include Maritime Museum or a playground

- **Highlights:** Explore Rotterdam in an interactive way, with games, puzzles, and scavenger hunts. Visit child-friendly attractions like the Maritime Museum or enjoy playtime in a park. Learn about Rotterdam's history in an engaging way for young minds.

8. **Rotterdam for History Buffs: World War II Walking Tour (Rotterdam Walks):** Step back in time and learn about Rotterdam's resilience during WWII with Rotterdam Walks.

    - **Location:** City Center (Meeting Point: De Doelen concert hall)

    - **End Point:** Near the reconstructed Sint Laurenskerk

    - **Highlights:** Explore remnants of the wartime bombings, discover stories of heroism and resistance, and learn about Rotterdam's reconstruction efforts that led to its modern architecture.

9. **Beyond the City Limits: Kinderdijk Windmill Tour (Daytrip with Dutch Tours):** Escape the city for a scenic day trip to Kinderdijk with Dutch Tours.

    - **Location:** Departure from Rotterdam City Center (Meeting Point specified upon booking)

    - **End Point:** Return to Rotterdam City Center

    - **Highlights:** Witness the UNESCO World Heritage Site of Kinderdijk, with its rows of iconic windmills. Learn about Dutch water management and the history of wind power. Enjoy the peaceful countryside surroundings.

CHAPTER FIVE

Top Restaurants in Rotterdam

Fine Dining Restaurants in Rotterdam

Rotterdam's culinary scene transcends its reputation for hearty Dutch fare. The city boasts a vibrant fine dining scene, offering exquisite flavors and impeccable service. So, dress up for an unforgettable evening and embark on a culinary adventure at one of these exceptional restaurants:

1. **Parkheuvel (Euro 140-225+ per person):**

   - **Location:** Het Park 18, 3014 BG Rotterdam, Netherlands

   - **Price:** Fine Dining (Euro 140-225+ per person)

   - **Menu:** Tasting menus with seasonal variations, focusing on innovative French cuisine with international influences.

   - **Cuisines:** French, International

   - **Meals:** Dinner (Tuesday-Saturday)

- **Features:** Two Michelin stars, impeccable service, elegant ambiance, stunning views of the park.

- **Description:** Parkheuvel is the epitome of fine dining in Rotterdam. Chef Erik van Loo boasts two Michelin stars for his mastery of French cuisine with a modern twist. Expect an unforgettable gastronomic journey with an ever-changing tasting menu showcasing the freshest seasonal ingredients. The elegant ambiance, impeccable service, and stunning views of the park complete the experience.

2. **FG Food Labs (Euro 85-150 per person):**

    - **Location:** Nieuwe Binnenweg 331, 3011 LP Rotterdam, Netherlands

    - **Price:** Fine Dining (Euro 85-150 per person)

    - **Menu:** Seasonal tasting menus with a focus on innovative and playful dishes.

    - **Cuisines:** Modern European

    - **Meals:** Dinner (Wednesday-Saturday)

    - **Features:** One Michelin star, creative and playful cuisine, warm and inviting atmosphere.

- **Description:** FG Food Labs offers an exciting take on fine dining. Chef François Geernewegen creates playful and innovative dishes that tantalize the taste buds. Expect an ever-changing tasting menu showcasing seasonal ingredients and global inspiration. The warm and inviting atmosphere makes FG Food Labs a delightful place to explore the boundaries of modern European cuisine.

3. **Restaurant Fitzgerald (Euro 75-125 per person):**

    - **Location:** Gelderseplein 49, 3011 WD Rotterdam, Netherlands

    - **Price:** Fine Dining (Euro 75-125 per person)

    - **Menu:** À la carte menu and seasonal tasting menus featuring classic French dishes with a modern twist.

    - **Cuisines:** French

    - **Meals:** Dinner (Tuesday-Saturday)

    - **Features:** Art Deco ambiance, attentive service, extensive wine list.

- **Description:** Step back in time to the glamour of the Art Deco era at Restaurant Fitzgerald. The elegant setting and attentive service provide the perfect backdrop to savor classic French dishes with a modern touch. An à la carte menu and seasonal tasting menus offer a variety of choices, while the extensive wine list ensures the perfect pairing for every dish.

4. **Jamie van der Leeden (Euro 95-175 per person):**

   - **Location:** Westmaasstraat 15, 3013 AL Rotterdam, Netherlands

   - **Price:** Fine Dining (Euro 95-175 per person)

   - **Menu:** À la carte menu and tasting menus showcasing modern Dutch cuisine with a focus on local and seasonal ingredients.

   - **Cuisines:** Modern Dutch

   - **Meals:** Dinner (Tuesday-Saturday)

   - **Features:** Warm and inviting atmosphere, focus on fresh local ingredients, creative presentation.

- **Description:** Experience the heart of Dutch cuisine with a modern twist at Jamie van der Leeden. Chef Jamie van der Leeden creates artfully presented dishes that showcase the bounty of the Netherlands. The focus on fresh, local, and seasonal ingredients ensures an exceptional dining experience. The warm and inviting atmosphere makes Jamie van der Leeden a perfect place to enjoy a leisurely dinner.

Local Eats Gems You Won't Want to Miss

Forget fancy tablecloths and Michelin stars. Rotterdam's true culinary spirit lies in its local eats scene. Dive into a world of fresh flavors, friendly vibes, and hidden gems that capture the essence of this vibrant city. Here are 5 local eats restaurants guaranteed to tantalize your taste buds and leave you wanting more:

1. **Stalles** (Various Locations - Budget Friendly):

    - **Location:** Multiple locations throughout Rotterdam (find them at street markets or squares)

    - **Price:** Budget-friendly (Expect to pay around €5-€10 per dish)

- **Menu:** Rotating selection of local Dutch specialties like "Frikandel" (deep-fried sausage snack), "Bitterballen" (savory meatball), "Stroopwafel" (syrup waffle), and "Poffertjes" (mini pancakes).

- **Cuisines:** Dutch Street Food

- **Meals:** All Day

- **Features:** Grab-and-go convenience, perfect for a quick bite between sightseeing, friendly atmosphere.

- **Description:** Immerse yourself in the heart of Rotterdam's street food culture with a visit to a "Stalles." These food stalls, often found at markets or squares, offer a delightful hodgepodge of Dutch delicacies. From savory snacks like "Frikandel" to sweet treats like "Stroopwafel," these bites are the perfect way to sample local flavors on the go.

2. **De Ballentent** (Hoogstraat 31a, 3011 PM Rotterdam - Budget Friendly):

    - **Location:** Hoogstraat 31a, 3011 PM Rotterdam, Netherlands

- **Price:** Budget-friendly (Expect to pay around €5-€10 per dish)

- **Menu:** Specializes in "Gehaktballen" (Dutch meatballs) with various toppings and sauces.

- **Cuisines:** Dutch

- **Meals:** Lunch and Dinner (Closed on Sundays)

- **Features:** Casual and cozy ambiance, limited seating (be prepared for a short wait), focus on one dish done exceptionally well.

- **Description:** "De Ballentent" translates to "The Meatball Tent," and that's exactly what it is! This Rotterdam institution offers a simple yet delicious menu centered around the mighty "Gehaktbal." Choose from classic or adventurous toppings, with a variety of sauces to complement your perfect meatball experience. The casual ambiance and focus on one dish done exceptionally well make "De Ballentent" a must-try for any local eats enthusiast.

3. **Backyard (Witte de Withstraat 74, 3012 BG Rotterdam - Mid-Range):**

- **Location:** Witte de Withstraat 74, 3012 BG Rotterdam, Netherlands

- **Price:** Mid-range (Expect to pay around €15-€25 per dish)

- **Menu:** Vegetarian and Vegan-friendly, with a focus on healthy and innovative plant-based dishes like burgers, salads, bowls, and smoothies.

- **Cuisines:** Vegetarian, Vegan

- **Meals:** Lunch and Dinner (Closed on Mondays)

- **Features:** Industrial-chic ambiance, extensive vegan menu with creative options, focus on fresh and sustainable ingredients.

- **Description:** Catering to the city's health-conscious crowd, Backyard offers a vibrant and delicious vegetarian and vegan menu. From their signature "Pulled No Chicken" burger made with oyster mushrooms to their power-packed smoothies, Backyard proves that plant-based food can be exciting and satisfying. The industrial-chic ambiance creates a trendy and welcoming atmosphere.

4. **Aloha** (Nieuwe Binnenweg 74, 3011 LP Rotterdam - Mid-Range):

- **Location:** Nieuwe Binnenweg 74, 3011 LP Rotterdam, Netherlands

- **Price:** Mid-range (Expect to pay around €15-€25 per dish)

    - **Menu:** Surinamese cuisine with a focus on flavorful curries, stews, and roti wraps.

- **Cuisines:** Surinamese

- **Meals:** Lunch and Dinner (Closed on Mondays)

- **Features:** Warm and inviting atmosphere, friendly service, generous portions.

- **Description:** Rotterdam boasts a rich multicultural tapestry, reflected in its diverse food scene. Aloha offers an authentic taste of Suriname, a former Dutch colony in South America. Expect flavorful curries, stews, and roti wraps bursting with bold spices and fresh ingredients.

Bites That Won't Break the Bank

Rotterdam may be a modern metropolis, but delicious and affordable eats are always within reach. Forget expensive sit-down meals – explore the city's vibrant food scene with these 5 budget-friendly bites restaurants that offer big flavors without a hefty price tag:

1. **Kapsalon (Various Locations - Budget Friendly):**

    - **Location:** Multiple locations throughout Rotterdam (find them in snack bars or food courts)

    - **Price:** Budget-friendly (Expect to pay around €5-€8)

    - **Menu:** A Rotterdam specialty – a layered dish of french fries, döner kebab meat, shawarma or shoarma (marinated grilled meat), melted cheese, and garlic sauce.

    - **Cuisines:** Dutch Fusion

    - **Meals:** All Day

    - **Features:** Quick and filling, perfect for a satisfying on-the-go meal, vegetarian options available.

- **Description:** A true Rotterdam icon, the Kapsalon (Dutch for "hairdresser") is a delightful explosion of textures and flavors. This layered masterpiece combines crispy fries, savory meats, gooey cheese, and a tangy garlic sauce. Vegetarian options are also available, making this a budget-friendly bite for everyone.

2. **FEBO (Various Locations - Budget Friendly):**

   - **Location:** Multiple locations throughout Rotterdam (look for the red vending machines)

   - **Price:** Budget-friendly (Expect to pay around €2-€5 per item)

   - **Menu:** A Dutch fast-food chain with vending machines dispensing hot and cold snacks like "kroketten" (deep-fried ragout croquettes), "frikandel" (deep-fried sausage snack), "bitterballen" (savory meatballs), and "bamibal" (deep-fried peanut satay ball).

   - **Cuisines:** Dutch Fast Food

   - **Meals:** All Day

- **Features:** Convenient and quick, 24/7 service (perfect for late-night cravings!), a variety of hot and cold snacks.

- **Description:** FEBO is a Rotterdam institution, offering a quick and convenient way to grab a bite on the go. Their vending machines dispense a variety of hot and cold snacks, perfect for satisfying any craving at any time of day. From classic "kroketten" to savory "bitterballen," FEBO is a budget-friendly way to experience Dutch fast food at its finest.

3. **Aloha Poke Bar (Nieuwe Binnenweg 311, 3011 LP Rotterdam - Budget Friendly):**

    - **Location:** Nieuwe Binnenweg 311, 3011 LP Rotterdam, Netherlands

    - **Price:** Budget-friendly (Expect to pay around €10-€15 per poke bowl)

    - **Menu:** Poke bowls with a focus on fresh, healthy ingredients like marinated raw fish, vegetables, rice, and a variety of sauces.

    - **Cuisines:** Hawaiian

- **Meals:** Lunch and Dinner

- **Features:** Build-your-own concept, fresh and healthy ingredients, perfect for a light and satisfying meal.

- **Description:** For a healthy and budget-friendly option, look no further than Aloha Poke Bar. This trendy spot allows you to build your own poke bowl, choosing from a variety of marinated raw fish, fresh vegetables, and flavorful sauces. It's a delicious and light option for a quick lunch or dinner break.

4. **Little V (Witte de Withstraat 53, 3012 BG Rotterdam - Budget Friendly):**

   - **Location:** Witte de Withstraat 53, 3012 BG Rotterdam, Netherlands

   - **Price:** Budget-friendly (Expect to pay around €5-€10 per item)

   - **Menu:** Vegetarian and Vegan Vietnamese street food like "banh mi" (Vietnamese baguettes), "goi cuon" (fresh spring rolls), and vegetarian pho (noodle soup).

- **Cuisines:** Vietnamese Street Food (Vegetarian & Vegan)

- **Meals:** Lunch and Dinner (Closed on Mondays)

- **Features:** Casual and cozy ambiance, quick service, perfect for a light bite or a full meal.

- **Description:** Embark on a flavor adventure to Vietnam at Little V. This vegetarian and vegan street food haven offers delicious and authentic Vietnamese bites like "banh mi" with savory fillings and refreshing "goi cuon" spring rolls. The casual ambiance and quick service make it a perfect spot for a budget-friendly lunch or dinner.

Deliciously Cheap Eats You Can't Miss!

Rotterdam isn't just about iconic architecture and trendy bars – it's also a haven for budget-conscious foodies! Forget fancy prix fixe menus – dive into the heart of Rotterdam's vibrant food scene with these 5 cheap eats restaurants offering big flavor without a hefty price tag:

1. **Shibuya (Nieuwe Binnenweg 240, 3011 LP Rotterdam):**

    - **Location:** Nieuwe Binnenweg 240, 3011 LP Rotterdam, Netherlands

    - **Price:** Super Cheap (Expect to pay around €5-€8 per dish)

    - **Menu:** Authentic Japanese street food favorites like "takoyaki" (savory octopus balls), "okonomiyaki" (savory pancakes), and "gyoza" (dumplings), all made fresh to order.

    - **Cuisines:** Japanese Street Food

    - **Meals:** Lunch and Dinner (Closed on Mondays)

    - **Features:** Casual and lively atmosphere, open kitchen, friendly service.

    - **Description:** Transport yourself to the streets of Tokyo at Shibuya. This tiny restaurant offers a delightful selection of Japanese street food classics made fresh to order right before your eyes. From the savory goodness of "takoyaki" to the satisfying bite of "gyoza," Shibuya is a budget-friendly adventure for your taste buds.

2. **Eetbar de Machinist (Proveniersplein 1, 3013 CP Rotterdam):**

- **Location:** Proveniersplein 1, 3013 CP Rotterdam, Netherlands

- **Price:** Super Cheap (Expect to pay around €5-€10 per dish)

- **Menu:** Rotterdam-style "broodje" (sandwiches) piled high with fresh ingredients and unique flavor combinations.

- **Cuisines:** Dutch (Sandwiches)

- **Meals:** Lunch

- **Features:** Local favorite, limited seating, perfect for a quick and satisfying lunch.

- **Description:** Experience Rotterdam's love affair with sandwiches at Eetbar de Machinist. This local favorite is renowned for its towering "broodjes" overflowing with fresh meats, cheeses, vegetables, and creative sauces. With friendly service and a quick turnaround, it's the perfect spot to grab a satisfying and affordable lunch.

3. **Falafel King (Witte de Withstraat 84, 3012 BG Rotterdam):**

   - **Location:** Witte de Withstraat 84, 3012 BG Rotterdam, Netherlands

   - **Price:** Super Cheap (Expect to pay around €5-€7 per wrap)

   - **Menu:** Authentic falafel wraps and bowls packed with fresh ingredients and flavorful sauces. Vegetarian and vegan options available.

   - **Cuisines:** Middle Eastern

   - **Meals:** Lunch and Dinner

   - **Features:** Quick service, generous portions, vegetarian and vegan options.

   - **Description:** Falafel King serves up a taste of the Middle East at a price that can't be beat. Their falafel wraps and bowls are overflowing with fresh falafel balls, crisp vegetables, creamy hummus, and tangy sauces. Vegetarian and vegan options ensure everyone can enjoy a delicious and affordable meal.

4. **Suraserie Makassar (Schiedamseweg 74A, 3011 EE Rotterdam):**

   - **Location:** Schiedamseweg 74A, 3011 EE Rotterdam, Netherlands

   - **Price:** Cheap (Expect to pay around €8-€12 per dish)

   - **Menu:** Indonesian cuisine with a focus on noodle soups like "bakso" (meatball soup) and "mie ayam" (chicken noodle soup), and rice dishes like "nasi goreng" (fried rice).

   - **Cuisines:** Indonesian

   - **Meals:** Lunch and Dinner

   - **Features:** Casual and family-friendly atmosphere, large portions, authentic flavors.

   - **Description:** Embark on a culinary adventure to Indonesia at Suraserie Makassar. This family-friendly restaurant offers a wide variety of Indonesian dishes, from steaming noodle soups to flavorful rice plates. The large portions and authentic flavors make it a budget-friendly way to experience Indonesian cuisine at its best.

Bars & Pubs for Every Mood

Rotterdam's nightlife scene is as diverse and vibrant as its architecture. From lively pubs to hidden cocktail gems, there's a perfect spot for every taste. So, raise a glass and explore these 5 unique bars and pubs that will quench your thirst and leave you wanting more:

1. **Paddy Murphy's Irish Pub (Rodezand 15, 3011 AA Rotterdam):**

    - **Location:** City Center (Near Blaak Station)

    - **Price:** Mid-range (Expect to pay around €5-€8 per drink)

    - **Menu:** Extensive beer selection with a focus on Irish classics like Guinness and Kilkenny, as well as a wide range of whiskeys. Pub fare like burgers, fish & chips, and Irish stews is also available.

    - **Cuisines:** Irish Pub Fare

    - **Features:** Authentic Irish pub atmosphere with live music on weekends, friendly staff, great place to watch sports games.

- **Description:** For a taste of the Emerald Isle, head to Paddy Murphy's. This lively pub boasts a warm and welcoming atmosphere, complete with Guinness on tap, a wide selection of whiskeys, and friendly banter. Live music on weekends adds to the lively atmosphere, making it a great place to unwind and catch a game.

2. **Wunderbar (Boomgaardsstraat 71, 3012 XR Rotterdam):**

    - **Location:** Oude Noorden (Near Museum Boijmans Van Beuningen)

    - **Price:** Mid-range (Expect to pay around €6-€9 per drink)

    - **Menu:** Creative and expertly crafted cocktails, a curated selection of craft beers, and an impressive wine list. Bar snacks are also available.

    - **Cuisines:** Bar Snacks

    - **Features:** Hip and trendy atmosphere, knowledgeable bartenders, outdoor seating, regular DJ nights.

- **Description:** Wunderbar is a haven for cocktail enthusiasts. Their talented bartenders create innovative and delicious cocktails using fresh ingredients and premium spirits. The hip and trendy atmosphere, with occasional DJ nights, makes it a perfect spot for a sophisticated night out.

3. **De Witte Aap (Witte de Withstraat 78, 3012 BG Rotterdam):**

    - **Location:** Kunsthal Area (Popular nightlife district)

    - **Price:** Mid-range (Expect to pay around €5-€8 per drink)

    - **Menu:** Extensive beer selection with local and international options, a good selection of wines, and classic cocktails.

    - **Cuisines:** N/A (Bar Snacks Available)

    - **Features:** Local hangout with a relaxed atmosphere, large outdoor seating area, perfect for people-watching.

    - **Description:** De Witte Aap, meaning "The White Monkey," is a Rotterdam institution. This popular bar attracts a diverse crowd with its relaxed atmosphere, extensive beer list, and friendly service. The large outdoor seating area is perfect for people-watching on the bustling Witte de Withstraat.

4. **Panenka (Eendrachtsweg 25, 3012 LB Rotterdam):**

   - **Location:** Feijenoord (Near De Kuip Stadium)

   - **Price:** Mid-range (Expect to pay around €5-€8 per drink)

   - **Menu:** Extensive selection of beers on tap and in bottles, a good wine list, and classic cocktails. Sports bar fare like burgers, wings, and nachos is also available.

   - **Cuisines:** Sports Bar Fare

   - **Features:** Lively sports bar atmosphere, large screens for watching games, great place to catch a match with friends.

   - **Description:** Calling all sports fans! Panenka is your ultimate game-day destination. This lively bar boasts a wide variety of beers, delicious food, and large screens for catching all the action. The energetic atmosphere and friendly staff make it a great place to cheer on your favorite team.

5. **Bird (Raampoortstraat 26, 3032 AJ Rotterdam):**

   - **Location:** Hofbogen (Underneath the old railway arches)

   - **Location:** Mid-range (Expect to pay around €6-€10 per drink)

   - **Menu:** Creative cocktails with a focus on fresh ingredients and seasonal flavors, a curated selection of craft beers, and a good wine list. Bar snacks are also available.

   - **Cuisines:** Bar Snacks

   - **Features:** Unique location under the railway arches, stylish and contemporary décor, live music events featuring various genres.

CHAPTER SIX

Day Trips from Rotterdam

Unveiling the Charms of Nearby Destinations

While Rotterdam captivates with its modern allure and bustling city life, the surrounding region unveils a plethora of day trip opportunities, inviting travelers to explore Dutch history, culture, and picturesque landscapes. Embark on unforgettable journeys to Delft, The Hague, Kinderdijk, and Gouda, just a short distance away from Rotterdam.

Delft

Immersing in Timeless Beauty: Step into the enchanting world of Delft, renowned for its scenic canals and historic architecture, as well as its famed Delftware pottery. Wander through the charming streets of the old town, adorned with gabled houses and unique boutiques. Visit iconic landmarks like the Oude Kerk and the Nieuwe Kerk, offering stunning vistas from their towers. Delve into the rich history of Delftware at the Royal Delft factory, witnessing the intricate craftsmanship and exploring its cultural significance in Dutch heritage.

The Hague

Exploring Regal Grandeur: Discover the regal allure of The Hague, the political capital of the Netherlands, boasting international importance and cultural landmarks. Explore the historic Binnenhof, delve into the architectural grandeur of the Peace Palace, and immerse yourself in art and history at the Mauritshuis. Enjoy a leisurely stroll along the picturesque Scheveningen beach, indulging in seaside delights amidst breathtaking scenery.

Kinderdijk

Witnessing Iconic Landmarks: Venture into the Dutch countryside to witness the iconic windmills of Kinderdijk, a UNESCO World Heritage site symbolizing the Netherlands' historic battle against water. Marvel at the 19 meticulously preserved windmills, set amidst polders and canals. Explore the area by boat or bicycle, uncovering the engineering marvels and historical significance behind these majestic structures.

Gouda

Delighting in Historic Charm: Delight in the historic charm of Gouda, a picturesque town celebrated for its cheese, scenic canals, and striking Gothic architecture. Visit landmarks such as the Gouda City Hall and the Markt square, and marvel at the captivating St. Janskerk adorned with mesmerizing stained glass windows. Savor the world-famous Gouda cheese at the Cheese Market, a quintessential experience during the summer months, and wander through streets lined with charming cheese shops and boutiques.

These enchanting destinations of Delft, The Hague, Kinderdijk, and Gouda offer a glimpse into the rich cultural heritage and scenic wonders of the Netherlands. So, take a break from the city bustle of Rotterdam and embark on these unforgettable day trips, where hidden treasures, Dutch traditions, and lasting memories await amidst captivating surroundings.

CONCLUSION

Unveiling Rotterdam's Unforgettable Spirit

This exploration of Rotterdam has taken you on a journey through a city that pulsates with innovation and embraces its rich history. We began by unveiling Rotterdam's essence – a place where cutting-edge architecture seamlessly blends with historical landmarks (Introduction). We delved into the city's must-see sights, from the iconic Markthal to the majestic Erasmus Bridge (Chapter Three).

Chapter One empowered you to plan your perfect Rotterdam adventure, offering tips on navigating the city and suggesting vibrant neighborhoods to explore. We also provided a comprehensive guide to finding the ideal accommodation, whether you seek luxurious comfort or budget-friendly options (Chapter Two).

To ensure you don't miss a beat, Chapter Four highlighted captivating tours that delve deeper into Rotterdam's hidden gems. Finally, Chapter Five tantalized your taste buds with a curated selection of top restaurants, catering to every budget and craving.

Rotterdam is a city that defies expectations, constantly evolving while cherishing its past. This book has equipped you with the knowledge and inspiration to embark on your own Rotterdam adventure. Whether you crave cultural immersion, architectural marvels, or a vibrant culinary scene, Rotterdam offers an unforgettable experience.

So, pack your bags, embrace the city's dynamic spirit, and discover why Rotterdam should be your next adventure!

With love

from

Betty Vanslyke

MyJournal

Title: _____ Date: _____

MyJournal

Title: _____ Date: _____

MyJournal

Title: _____   Date: _____

MyJournal

Title: _____   Date: _____

MyJournal

Title: _____ Date: _____

MyJournal

Title: _____   Date: _____

MyJournal

Title: _____ Date: _____

MyJournal

Title: _____   Date: _____

MyJournal

Title: _____   Date: _____

MyJournal

Title: _____ Date: _____

Printed in Great Britain
by Amazon